DESIGNING ORGANISATIONS

DESIGNING ORGANISATIONS

The foundation for excellence

PHILIP SADLER

MERCURY

First published in 1991
by Mercury Books
Gold Arrow Publications Limited,
862 Garratt Lane, London SW17 0NB

Set in Palatino by
Phoenix Photosetting, Chatham, Kent
Printed and bound in Great Britain by
Mackays of Chatham PLC, Chatham, Kent

British Library Cataloguing in Publication Data
Sadler, Philip 1930–
    Designing organisations.
    1. Organisations. Design, Management
    I. Title
    658.4

    ISBN 1–85251–088–9

Contents

'Thus we know pretty definitely the factors that make organization. They are structure, lines of authority, responsibility, division of labour, system, discipline, accounting, records and statistics; and *esprit de corps*, cooperation, "team play", but when we attempt to determine the parts played by these factors, we find that their relative importance changes with purpose, conditions and material. We begin to realize that there is an art of organizing that requires knowledge of aims, processes, men and conditions as well as of the principles of organization.'

Russell Robb, *Lectures on Organization* (1910, privately printed).

Organisation as Social Architecture

My co-authors and I downplayed the importance of structure in *In Search of Excellence* and again in *A Passion for Excellence*. We were terribly mistaken. Good intentions and brilliant proposals will be dead-ended, delayed, sabotaged, massaged to death, or revised beyond recognition or usefulness by the overlayered structures at most large and all too many small firms.

Tom Peters, *Thriving on Chaos*

Introduction

It is 8.30 am at Heathrow Airport, London. Intending BA passengers for the 10.00 am flight to Paris are checking in at a number of desks, each manned by a check-in clerk who has been well trained not only in the procedures to be followed but, equally important in the eyes of the airline's chief executive Colin Marshall, in customer service. The clerk is using a highly developed seat reservation and ticketing system which produces boarding passes and eliminates much traditional clerical work. Elsewhere in the airport a Boeing 737 is being prepared for departure. This involves a number of different activities – engineering, in-flight catering, refuelling, cleaning and security – and some of these in turn involve close collaboration between BA staff and employees of other organisations. The passengers' baggage is moved into the aircraft by the baggage handling crew while the passengers move into the departure lounge and are kept in touch with departure time and gate number by the airport's information system, which is fed updated information by BA staff. The flight crew is gathering for its briefing and also the cabin crew. At 9.30 am boarding commences. A fully serviceable aircraft, cleaned, refuelled, provisioned with an amazingly wide range of food and beverages as well as newspapers, magazines, medical supplies and blankets, waits at the appropriate gate, fully manned with highly trained personnel on the flight deck and in the cabin (despite the fact that it is winter, there is a flu epidemic and over 10 per cent of the airline's employees are absent due to sickness). At more or less precisely 10.00 am the aircraft moves away from its station and the flight commences.

The front-line personnel involved in this operation come from a wide range of departments and functions. They all know what they have to do, how best to do it, when to do it and with whom to liaise. They could not do their jobs without the support of accountants, buyers, computer specialists, design teams, employee relations specialists, health and safety specialists, legal experts, office workers of all kinds, planners, public relations officers, personnel managers, safety experts, trainers and a host of others.

The successful take-off on time is a small miracle. It will be repeated many more times the same day at

Heathrow and at other airports in far countries. This can happen only because BA has developed a highly effective organisation, one that gets the job done efficiently, motivates its employees, meets or even exceeds its customers' expectations and provides its shareholders with a satisfactory return on their capital.

The Origins of Organisation

One of the earliest accounts of organisation design can be found in the Bible, in Exodus. Moses' father-in-law Jethro watched Moses sitting in judgement from morning to evening while the people of Israel patiently queued to present their petitions or register their complaints. He told Moses, 'The thing that thou doest is not good. Thou will surely wear away, both thou, and this people that is with thee; for this thing is too heavy for thee; thou art not able to perform it thyself alone.' He then proposed that Moses should select able men to be rulers of thousands, rulers of hundreds, rulers of fifties and rulers of tens. Every great decision should still be brought to Moses but otherwise these leaders should judge and decide the smaller affairs. Moses accepted Jethro's advice and from that time his task of leading the tribes of Israel to the Promised Land was eased.

For thousands of years since, mankind has designed and developed organisations in order to control and co-ordinate the activities of large numbers of people in relation to some common task. Until relatively recently large complex organisations existed mainly in three spheres – the state, the army and the Church. With industrialisation, however, came a new type of purposive human grouping: the industrial organisation, with its new types of activity and with its very foundation resting on a newly articulated principle of organisation design – the division of labour.

Adam Smith (1922), writing in *The Wealth of Nations*, takes as the classic example the trade of pin-making, pointing out that one skilled worker doing the whole job could perhaps make one pin per day. In a manufacturing organisation, however,

one man draws the wire, another straightens it, a third cuts it, a fourth points it, a fifth grinds it at the top for receiving the head; to make the head requires two or three distinct operations; to put it on is a peculiar business, to whiten the pins is another; it is even a trade by itself to put them into the paper; and the important business of making a pin is, in this manner, divided into about eighteen distinct operations, which, in some manufactories, are all performed by distinct hands, though in others the same man will sometimes perform two or three of them. I have seen a small manufactory of this kind where ten men only were employed . . . they could, when they exerted themselves, make among them about twelve pounds of pins in a day. There are in a pound upwards of four thousand pins of a middling size. Those ten persons, therefore, could make among them upwards of forty eight thousand pins in a day. Each person, therefore, making a tenth part of forty eight thousand pins might be considered as making four thousand eight hundred pins in a day. But if they had all wrought separately and independently they could certainly not each of them have made twenty, perhaps not one pin in a day.

Since Adam Smith's time industrial and commercial organisations have developed considerably. They have grown in size – Britain's largest industrial employer, British Telecom, employs 234,000 people, the US giant General Motors has a turnover in excess of $65 billion. Functional specialisation has increased enormously. Corporations have moved across national boundaries – IBM operates in over 100 countries. They have developed ranges of products or services from an initial simple starting point. They frequently serve quite different markets, selling their products to governments, other industrial corporations and to various categories of consumers.

Simultaneously, the basic functions of government have multiplied, bringing into existence massive and complex organisations in fields such as education, health and social services. The British National Health Service employs a million people and spends £6 billion annually on procurement.

The development of these powerful instruments of purpose has made possible the living standards of the developed countries of the world. Important as specific advances in science and technology have been, it is the harnessing of technology through organisation which transforms productivity and raises living standards. For economic progress to take place it is obviously important to know how to do such things as generate electricity, make cement, design and build machine tools, preserve foodstuffs or carry out calculations faster than the human brain can comprehend. Yet none of these pieces of knowledge can be exploited without organisation, and the problems that must be solved in designing effective organisations are every bit as complex as those involved in designing machines. These problems have attracted the interest of some powerful intellects,

[5]

working in the social rather than the natural sciences.

In the early years of the twentieth century writers such as Max Weber, Lyndall Urwick, Elton Mayo, Chester Barnard and many others have explored the complex issues involved in organisation design and illuminated them to a considerable extent. In more recent years, following a more empirical approach, researchers in the business schools and universities such as Alfred Chandler, Joan Woodward, Michel Crozier, Paul Lawrence, Jay Lorsch and John Child have attempted to engage in comparative studies of effective and less effective organisations and to arrive at valid generalisations about organisation design from such comparisons. Remarkably few writers have, however, tried to distill the essence of this analysis and research for the benefit of managers faced with making decisions about organisation. This book is an attempt to fill this gap.

Above all, it is written for the manager who is driven by the strong need to build an organisation of which he or she can be justly proud, one which is simultaneously effective on several fronts. Tom Peters has used the expression 'A passion for excellence' as the title for one of his highly stimulating books. At first sight it may seem strange to link the idea of passion with something as abstract as organisation theory. Yet there can be few tasks in life as potentially rewarding and fulfilling as leading fulfilled human beings in the accomplishment of worthwhile goals.

Organisational Effectiveness

It is virtually impossible to define organisational effectiveness without making highly debatable value judgements, so instead of ducking the question of values it is better to tackle them head-on by examining the way in which different 'stakeholders' might value an organisation and so be prepared to describe it as effective.

Shareholders, for example, would tend to describe as effective an organisation whose consistently above average profitability and growth resulted in an increase in the share price. Employees might take a different view and emphasise the extent to which the organisation was 'a good employer' – paying good wages, providing good working conditions, scope for satisfying work and security of employment. Customers would naturally focus on things to do with value for money, quality and reliability of goods, courtesy of service, punctuality of delivery. Suppliers would emphasise fair prices and prompt payment. Each viewpoint is valid but partial, in the sense that the ability to satisfy any one group of stakeholders is, in the medium to long term at least, dependent on the organisation's ability to satisfy all the others. Profits depend on satisfied customers. To satisfy customers without motivated employees or satisfactory relationships with suppliers is unlikely to be possible for very long.

Organisational effectiveness is, therefore, many-faceted. It involves not only achieving outstanding levels of performance relative to the competition but also keeping in balance the expectations of the various groups of people involved. Marks and Spencer is an example of an effective organisation in this sense, giving a strong performance in profitable growth leading to its being regarded as a blue chip investment prospect on the stock market; its emphasis on good human relations and pay and working conditions leads to high commitment and motivation on the part of the workforce; the customers are plainly very satisfied; and many suppliers have been rescued from bankruptcy not only by the contracts offered to them by Marks and Spencer but also by the practical help the retailing giant has given in raising their productivity and quality.

Effectiveness in the Public Sector

Clearly one cannot judge the excellence of a state school or university or a charity on profitability criteria. The same principles of analysis can, however, be applied.

To take a school as an example, the 'customers' are clearly the children and their parents. The determinants of overall satisfaction will be complex and will include examination results, the level of sporting achievements, the 'social climate' of the school and the standard of discipline maintained, as well as other features. The employees include not only the teachers, whose level of commitment to the goals of the school will be vital, but also the administrative and catering staff. The final stakeholder is the taxpayer, who will look for evidence of a satisfactory rate of return on the public expenditure involved and for indications that the material and human resources available to the school are being effectively used. A newly appointed headmaster or headmistress seeking to build an outstandingly success-ful school on the foundations of one of merely average accomplishments should be able to utilise the greater part of the ideas in this book.

Perceptions of Organisation

As with so many other aspects of our world, what you see when you look at an organisation depends on your perspective – on where you are coming from. If you are the chairman or chief executive your perspective is likely to be particularly subject to distortion. This is partly due to the same kind of blindness as the natural pride in their children that causes parents to regard their offspring as beautiful people endowed with intelligence and all the human virtues. It is partly due to the blindness of familiarity: you walk up the path to the front door of the headquarters building every day and do not notice, as a stranger would, that it is badly in need of a coat of paint. And it partly reflects the fact that however 'open' you try to make the organisation people will tend to give you the good news and shield you from the bad; they will tidy up if they know you are coming; they are unlikely to have their feet on the desks reading newspapers if they know you are prowling the office.

What are some of the other perspectives that can be important? Some are obviously to be found inside the organisation – the perspectives of employees at different levels and in different parts of it. Knowing what these perspectives are is vitally important for top management yet surprisingly few firms make systematic efforts to find out. Perhaps the most notable exception is IBM, which regularly carries out opinion and attitude surveys among its employees and cannot envisage managing without them. In 1964 an American arrived at Greenock in Scotland to take over management of the IBM manufacturing plant there. He telephoned the personnel director of IBM (UK) in London. 'Where are the employee opinion survey data?' he asked. 'We don't do opinion surveys in Britain', he was told. 'How can I possibly run a plant if I don't know what the employees are thinking? I want a survey done and I want it done now.' So the first Greenock opinion survey was carried out in 1964 and has been repeated every two years or so since then. In a part of Britain previously characterised by poor employee relations and strikes, Greenock has developed to be one of IBM's most productive and high-quality plants worldwide.

There are other important perspectives from outside, or from a position on the boundary which separates the organisation from its environment. Do you know how your organisation is perceived by:

- Its customers? (If not, it's surprising you are still in business!)

- Young graduates in their last year of university, looking for a job?

- Young school-leavers in your locality?

- The chief planning officer of your local authority?

- Pressure groups concerned with such issues as equal opportunity, environmental conservation, facilities for the disabled?

- The local and national press?

- Investment analysts in the City?

- Investors, especially fund managers?

- Its bankers?

- Its major suppliers of materials and components?

- Relevant departments of national and foreign governments?

- Relevant trade unions?

- Main competitors?

It is important to bear in mind how these perceptions are developed. It is also important to note that once they have been developed they are very difficult to change. Some of the factors that influence perceptions of an organisation from the outside include:

- the quality, reliability and value for money of the goods or services;

- the approach, appearance and attitude of the organisation's representatives who deal with the outside world;

- the standard of repair, aesthetic qualities and other characteristics (Are they surrounded by landscaped gardens, for example, or rubbish tips?) of the organisation's premises;

- the various communications observable by visitors coming to the organisation (Are there reserved parking spaces for visitors? Are they closer to the building than those reserved for staff? Does the top management team have personally named parking spaces? Is the reception area welcoming, with flowers, magazines, comfortable seating, and the like?);

[11]

- the cleanliness of the organisation's vehicles and the standard of behaviour of the drivers;

- news reports about the organisation's activities;

- the quality and nature of the design of the organisation's stationery, printed materials, packaging, etc.

Probably the least effective ways of forming perceptions are the organisation's own deliberate attempts to do so by means of corporate (as distinct from product) advertising campaigns. A classic British example was British Rail's 'We're getting there' campaign, which was a mere whisper in the face of the thunder of communication in the form of late, dirty and overcrowded trains, rude and untidily dressed staff, and dirty and decaying stations.

A full assessment of the organisation's strengths and weaknesses and its potential for development and growth needs to be based as far as possible on information from all relevant sources.

The Objectives of Organisation Design

Clearly the overall objective is to create an effective organisation, as previously defined. Within this broad objective, however, some important sub-goals can be identified.

- Achieving the appropriate level of *control* over the activities of members of the organisation.

- Achieving an adequate degree of *co-ordination* and *integration* of people's activities in relation to the organisation's overall purpose.

- Providing necessary and effective interfaces with key aspects of the organisation's *environment*: in particular, with customers and the market; with local and central government; with key suppliers; with pressure groups; with trade unions; and with the media and community leaders.

- Influencing *motivation* and *commitment* to the organisation's goals on the part of its members.

- Achieving *innovation* and *flexibility* – the capacity to respond quickly to the need to change.

Each of these sub-goals will be discussed in a separate chapter.

That the demands of these sub-goals will often be in conflict is obvious. The need for close control may be in conflict with the need for job satisfaction, for example. In such cases priorities must be set and compromises accepted.

The Basic Elements of Organisation

It can be useful to employ biological analogies when describing organisational characteristics. For example, structure can be compared to the anatomy of an organism, systems and procedures to the physiology, and values and culture to its mental and emotional

[13]

states. The design of organisations encompasses all three of these aspects.

Structure defines such things as formal channels for reporting and issuing instructions and the allocation of authority and responsibility. It also involves the deployment of what Bartlett and Ghoshal (1989) call 'micro-structural tools' such as task forces and project groups.

Systems and procedures consist of a wide range of laid-down methods for information processing, decision-making and taking action. These are formalised to differing degrees in different organisations, but some information exchange, decision-making and activities will take place informally in all organisations, using procedures that have never been written down and networks that are not officially recognised.

Values and culture may also be more or less formalised. Mission statements exemplify the more formal approach and are common in Japanese companies, less so in US corporations and are least often found in European businesses. Culture can be influenced in many other ways, however, such as role-modelling by top management, personnel policies and decisions about structure and systems.

Figure 1 shows how structural characteristics, choice of systems and procedures and the development of cultural features of organisation can be used to achieve the different objectives of organisation design.

Roles

As a member of an organisation a person does more than fill a job; he or she occupies a *role*.

[14]

	STRUCTURE	SYSTEM	CULTURE
CONTROL	HIERARCHY AND SPAN OF CONTROL	PRODUCTION CONTROL, STOCK CONTROL, ETC.	BUREAUCRATIC OR MECHANISTIC
CO-ORDINATION AND INTEGRATION	PRODUCT DIVISIONALISATION, MATRIX STRUCTURES	INTEGRATED MANUFACTURING SYSTEMS	TEAMWORKING
ENVIRONMENTAL 'FIT'	MARKET OR GEOGRAPHICAL DIVISIONS, BOUNDARY ROLES	ENVIRONMENTAL SCANNING SYSTEMATIC CONSUMER RESEARCH	OUTWARD LOOKING, MARKET ORIENTED
MOTIVATION	AUTONOMOUS WORK GROUPS JOB ENRICHMENT	INCENTIVE SCHEMES EMPLOYEE SHARE OWNERSHIP SCHEMES	PUTTING PEOPLE FIRST
FLEXIBILITY/INNOVATION	FLAT STRUCTURES DECENTRALISATION PROJECT GROUPS	GENESIS GRANTS 15 PER CENT RULE	ENTREPRENEURIAL, ORGANIC

Figure 1   The elements of organisation

Designing Organisations

The difference can be explained by a simple example. A self-employed person with a particular set of skills or a particular profession – a bricklayer or an accountant – will have to perform certain activities to follow his or her trade or profession. These activities will often not be confined to the specific ones associated with that field of work: they can include such things as simple bookkeeping, some marketing, some simple administration. This is still a 'job', however, and not an organisation role.

Once the same person joins an organisation other behaviours will be expected of him or her. These expectations will come partly from the management (creating a formal role) and partly from co-workers (the informal role). One of the most common definitions of role is 'a set of expectations held by people who interact with the occupant of a particular position'.

Formal roles will not only specify the jobs to be done and certain other job-related behaviour but will also define other factors which are concerned with 'fitting-in' to the organisation rather than doing a particular job. These other factors may include such elements as:

- *Relationships*   A map of organisational relationships showing how the particular role should relate to others and indicating lines of reporting, co-worker relationships and group membership.

- *Rights and obligations*   A statement of rights and obligations: what the role incumbent is entitled to and what is expected of him or her – punctuality, for example, or a willingness to work overtime.

- *Dress and deportment*   A self-employed accountant can work as effectively in a T-shirt as in a business

[16]

suit. As a member of the accounts team in most major business organisations, however, if male he will be expected to wear a dark suit and sober tie.

- *Status*   The employee will find that his or her role inescapably involves enjoying (if that is an appropriate term) a position within a status system and that (in most organisations) very strong expectations about his or her behaviour will be associated with the perceptions others have of this status. If the person's status is at the lower end the expectations of others will be shattered if he or she addresses the chief executive using his or her first name, or parks right outside the main entrance to the headquarters building. If, on the other hand, the person's status is very high, expectations will be equally shattered if he or she is seen walking around the building eating an ice cream cone or playing poker with the maintenance crew during a rest break.

These aspects of the role may or may not be written down. Frequently they are not and new employees learn about them not only during induction processes but also, less formally and often quite painfully, from co-workers.

Designing an organisation involves more than designing jobs; it involves designing roles. Recruiting people involves filling roles as well as filling jobs.

Organisational Groupings

There are several ways of grouping people together in

organisations. With one exception, these apply at every level from the shop floor to the very top.

- *By function*   This category can be divided into two sub-groups:

  1. *Common qualifications*, e.g. an accounts department (all accountants) or a welding shop (all skilled welders). Members of such a group identify with a particular skills group as a trade or profession.

  2. *Performing closely allied tasks* in relation to the firm's overall goals but often mixed in respect of skills or qualifications. The manufacturing function, for example, may include not only skilled and unskilled workers, engineers, production supervisors and managers but, in a large manufacturing division, accountants, personnel people, medical and nursing staff, etc. They share an identification with a *business function* rather than a skill or membership of a profession.

- *By product, by service, by project*   The members of such a group may represent several different skills or professions and be drawn from various business functions. What binds them together is their focus on a particular outcome of their joint activity – a product line, a particular form of service or a task or project to be completed.

- *By market segment served*   Here the cement that binds the group together is a shared interest in a particular type of client being served. Examples

[18]

would include the administrative/medical/technical team running a geriatric hospital or a sales group that focuses on selling ethical drugs to the medical profession.

- *By area or territory*   Members of an area-based group may possess varied skills, deal with varied products, perform different business functions or serve different types of clients but what links them together is a feeling of belonging to a common locality – be it a region of a country or a country or a region of the world.

- *By time (shiftworkers)*   This last category does not apply at top level but is often important at work-group level in multi-shift plants where workers may identify themselves with particular shifts.

Ask any employee of an organisation to talk about his or her work and life in the organisation. Sooner or later he or she will be likely to give an unprompted insight into his or her group identification by saying such things as, 'I'm an accountant', 'I'm in sales', 'I work on computers', 'I work with handicapped children', 'I'm with Southern Region' or 'I work nights'.

Choices about how best to group people in order to optimise efficiency and motivation can be critical to a company's success. The choices are very wide; sometimes, but by no means always, they are constrained. They are not simple either/or choices. In a large complex organisation all these forms of grouping will be found. What is important is how they are combined and which are seen as most important. This issue will be explored further in Chapter 3.

What Factors Determine the Design of Organisations?

First, there are factors to do with people. At a general level the design of an organisation may reflect ideas about the forms of organisation that are most effective in mobilising human talent and energy. More specifically, the expressed wishes of organisation members may be taken into account or the design of the structure may reflect a desire to accommodate individuals' strengths and weaknesses. This approach emphasises the advantages of fitting the structure to the people rather than the people to the structure.

Second, there are factors concerning the situation facing the enterprise, such as strategy, technology and task. For example, if the business strategy involves diversification of the product range the structure chosen will almost certainly be different from that seen as appropriate to a strategy based on a 'stick to the knitting' philosophy. As Joan Woodward (1965) has demonstrated, the structure appropriate to the technology of mass production differs from that appropriate to the technologies of batch or continuous flow production. Task characteristics are also important; for example, tasks involving considerable risks to human safety will often call for more stringent control systems and hence different structural arrangements for control than tasks which have no safety implications.

Third, there are influences which reflect the scale and complexity of the organisation's activities. Large complex organisations need elaborate and highly sophisticated systems of organisation, unlike small organisations engaged in a very limited range of opera-

[20]

tions. Pugh (1973), for example, showed how size and other contextual factors influence the configuration of organisations.

Fourth, there are specific theories about organisation design which may be acquired by reading books, attending executive development programmes or hiring consultants, or be imported by senior executives from organisations in which they have worked previously and in which particular features of organisation design were associated with successful performance.

Finally, there are values, beliefs, and attitudes – cultural factors – which the decision-makers tend to share. These may be derived in part from the general cultural and social environment of the business (as is conspicuously the case with Japanese industry) or inherited from the organisation's own past experience. These values will affect such matters as the extent to which the organisation is hierarchical, the emphasis placed on status, the value placed on systems and procedures and the extent to which one business function (perhaps production) is seen as more important to the business than another (perhaps marketing). Values and beliefs are dangerous influences on organisation design since decision-makers are often unaware of the bias resulting from them. They may operate against the effective performance of tasks. For example, in the case of the London Life Insurance Company, Thompson-McCausland and Biddle (1985) relate how selling was almost a dirty word and the selling function enjoyed very low status. This value system disturbed the organisation structure and contributed to the company's declining fortunes.

Values and beliefs may not always influence organisation design beneficially but in practice may well exercise a stronger influence on decisions about organisation than any of the other factors that have been listed. Attempts to improve organisational effectiveness by introducing structures and systems based on careful analysis of the job to be done and the abilities and needs of the employees have often foundered when confronted with the resistance to change deriving from traditional sets of values and beliefs.

Organisation Diagnosis and Development

Very few managers have the opportunity to build an organisation from scratch. When taking up their appointments managers at all levels normally 'inherit' existing organisations. They then face two sets of issues. The first is that from time to time they should consider whether or not the organisation is appropriate, is functioning effectively, has adapted well to changing circumstances, or is in need of modification or even radical redesign. The second issue is rather different and reflects the need to make a major adjustment to the organisation as a result of an important change or event – examples include a merger with another organisation, relocation to new premises, the need to contract sharply in size following a business recession or the introduction of radically new technology.

This book is intended to help managers facing situations such as these and to offer them useful and practical guidance in diagnosing organisational problems and making decisions about organisation change and development as well as those in start-up situations.

Organisation as 'Social Architecture'

A distinction needs to be made between *organising* and *building an organisation*. Matters such as the allocation of tasks, the delegation of authority and systems for control are involved whenever the efforts of large numbers of people are co-ordinated in carrying out a common task. Organising, in this sense, is needed in many situations which do not involve building an organisation, for example in the case of a community clearing up after a hurricane, or – to take a historical example – slaves constructing a pyramid.

Building an organisation, however, involves things besides structures and methods of working. Above all it involves binding people together with a sense of belonging and a sense of common purpose continuing over time, and cementing the whole together with some shared values and ideals. It is a process of social architecture, of institution building. It is no coincidence that so many of the world's great business corporations – IBM, Marks and Spencer, 3M, Honda, Volvo and the like – have paid special attention to organisation building. For these companies, the creation of a human organisation aspiring to certain ideals has been a key objective. For them, organising in the narrower sense has no significance. This book is about the lessons that can be learned from such companies; it is about building effective organisations, not about organising.

2

Control

Introduction

To be in control of something means to be in possession of the relevant information and to have the ability or power to act, to get things done. In terms of organisational life, managers need to know what is happening at shop-floor level or out in the field and they need to be able to exercise the right amount of influence on what is happening in order to produce the desired results.

Control, therefore, has two aspects, which will be dealt with in sequence: information for control purposes and exercising control.

Information for Control Purposes

This in turn has two aspects to it: first, there is the need to decide what information is needed for control purposes; second, the implications of the information system for organisation design have to be thought through. For some theorists, such as March and Simon in the USA or Britain's Stafford Beer, the management information system is *the* central plank of organisational design. In *Brain of the Firm* Stafford Beer (1972) argues that cybernetics (the science of control and communication) offers new insights into the problems of large complex systems such as industrial organisations, and he presents a study of organisation and its problems based on the human nervous system. The system that provides information for control purposes is undeniably important; it is also true that in many enterprises insufficient consideration is given to it. In the last analysis, however, it is just one aspect of the overall design task and must be balanced against the demands of the other factors.

The design of the information system does, nevertheless, offer a useful starting point for the overall task of organisation design, since it is pointless to begin to create an information system without first having a clear idea of the functioning of the organisation as a whole and the way in which different activities come together in relation to the whole. Without such a model it is difficult both to decide what key management information is required and to resolve many other organisational issues.

Thus, the best starting point for organisation design is the organisation's purpose and the particular strategies or objectives relating to that purpose. Since control cannot be exercised in a vacuum but only in relation to established standards or goals, the first practical step is to establish such standards. Given the objective of designing an organisation that is effective on a wide range of fronts, standards will need to be established under the following headings.

- *Internal efficiencies* Examples include profit on turnover, profit on capital employed, cash flows, levels of stocks and work in progress, productivity and quality of product.

- *Customer satisfaction*, involving matters such as percentage of complaints or goods returned, average waiting time on telephone calls and percentage of deliveries made on time.

- *Employee satisfaction*, including job satisfaction and organisational commitment as reflected in opinion surveys, labour turnover, and sickness and absenteeism.

- *Supplier satisfaction* and *satisfactoriness*: responses to surveys of suppliers' opinions, percentage of faults and rejections of components, etc.

This may seem elementary, yet how many boards of directors regularly receive information under the first heading only? If so, what makes them think they are in control of the business?

It is also important to distinguish between tactical controls, which tell us how the business is performing *currently*, and strategic controls, which tell us if the business is on course to achieve its *strategic* objectives. Strategic controls are more difficult to devise than tactical ones.

Strategic Controls

The organisational implications of having strategic controls in place may give rise to the need for special structural and procedural arrangements. Goold (1989) gives an excellent example of this, using the US corporation, General Electric.

By 1980 General Electric was both huge and highly diversified, with world sales exceeding $25 billion. This complex set of activities was managed through a structure having five levels:

- corporate office;

- sectors, e.g. power systems, industrial products, consumer products, international, etc.;

- groups, e.g. (within consumer products sector) major appliance group, lighting business group;

- divisions, e.g. (within lighting business group) lamp products division, lamp components division;

- departments, e.g. (within lamp components division) lamp glass products department, refractory metals products department, etc.

Overlaid on this line management structure was a *separate structure* for purposes of strategic planning. This focused on forty strategic business units (SBUs), which could be located at group, divisional or departmental levels and which cut across line management structures. SBUs were defined in terms of the major sources of competitive advantage and not in terms of the existing structure of authority and accountability in respect of operations. An SBU should have the ability to stand alone as a viable and completely successful independent company within its own market. Strategic plans were prepared annually for each SBU *as well as* for each major sector of the business as a whole. *Budgets included specific*

[27]

expense items associated with carrying out agreed strategic programmes. SBU budgets, however, had to be broken down into departmental budgets, with responsibility for implementation located in the regular operating hierarchy rather than in the strategic SBU structure. The structure proved to be too complex, however, and the corporation's next chief executive, Jack Welch, set out to reduce the complexity facing him, partly by portfolio rationalisation, but also by restructuring. The number of SBUs was reduced to fourteen, all of which reported directly to him in order to make it possible for the centre to be involved with the business on important aspects of strategy.

Designing Control Systems

Having set standards in all those areas of activity the next step involves asking such questions as:

- How *quickly* after the events it relates to do I need to have the information?

- How *frequently* do I need to have it?

- In what *format* do I want it? Figures? Charts? Written narrative? Verbal reporting?

  At this point there are some dangers to be avoided

- Do not confuse data (especially yards of computer print-out) with information.

- Do not get excited about recording history – concentrate on control information which indicates the directions of change and provides early warning signals about the future.

- Do not ignore the fact that some of the key information you need to run the business relates to what your competitors are doing (just as when in control of a car in traffic, information about what the drivers of other vehicles are doing is vital if you are to reach your destination safely). How many boards of directors *regularly* receive information about competitors' activities and performance?

Once the overall design of the control system has been delineated it is time to consider the implications for the rest of the structure. Questions that need to be faced include:

- Providing the information needed will have to form all or part of some people's jobs. Which jobs? To what extent should providing (and analysing) information become a specialised activity?

- Recording and processing information creates and consumes paper. Since paperwork stifles other activity, how can it be kept to a minimum consistent with obtaining the information you must have for control purposes?

- Information flows along channels of communication. In organisations such channels typically have 'valves' or 'filters', called levels in the hierarchy. What can be done to ensure that essential information reaches decision-makers promptly and undistorted?

- Feedback for control purposes is needed at *every* level of the organisation. If a guest in a hotel complains of a dirty room it is just as important for the chambermaid to have this information as it is for the general manager. How can the internal communication system be designed to provide adequate feedback at all levels?

- How can the system be designed to avoid giving employees the feeling that they are being spied on? (The tachometer is an ideal device for recording details of the movements of vehicles for control purposes. To long-distance lorry drivers or truckers it is known as 'the spy in the cab'.)

- What uses can be made of information technology to streamline the management information system and enhance the quality of decision-making? For example, a computer model of the business can be developed, based on known relationships between prices and volumes and other key variables. This can then be used in a variety of ways: to generate reports, to consolidate management information from different operating divisions or subsidiary companies, or to carry out sensitivity analysis – a process which makes it possible to vary input figures, such as prices, and investigate the results of such changes on various outputs, such as sales volume and profit.

Exercising Control

The design implications of information systems for control purposes cannot in practice be divorced from the

[30]

design implications of the way in which control is exercised, just as the use of information for control purposes when driving (speedometer, fuel and temperature gauges, feedback through the steering and suspension) cannot be separated from the exercise of control by means of the brakes, accelerator and steering.

Here, there are three basic questions to be answered.

1 How *much* control will achieve the desired objectives or standards of performance?
2 How is that control to be exercised?
3 What are the implications for organisation design?

The answer to the first question depends on a number of factors. First, is the activity capable of being closely specified and controlled? In the case of the specific procedure to be followed by a supermarket check-out operator the answer is clearly 'yes'. In the case of a researcher looking for a cure for AIDS the answer is clearly 'no'. The difficult areas, however, are the shades of grey in between.

Second, what effect is close control, or the opposite, likely to have on the motivation and job satisfaction of employees? The motivation of the more educated, creative, imaginative or rebellious will be adversely affected by close and tight control. Others may welcome it.

Third, is close control likely to result in adverse consequences by inhibiting flexibility of response during periods of rapid change?

Finally, are there special requirements for close control arising out of the fact that the activities in question involve high risk? Obvious examples include risks to health and safety, to security and those involved in handling large sums of money.

[31]

Designing Organisations

Means of Exercising Control

There is a number of possible ways of exercising control and the majority of large organisations will employ most or indeed all of these in combination.

A broad distinction can be made initially between control over inputs and control over outputs; in other words, controlling the way people do their jobs on the one hand and exercising control by looking at the results they achieve, on the other. In some organisations there is a bias towards close control over detailed activities in the belief that such an approach optimises results. Marks and Spencer in the UK provides a clear example of this approach. The duties of a store manager are laid down precisely and in great detail and the job leaves very little scope for discretion. In other organisations the bias is in the opposite direction, with a very strong focus on results and relatively little concern with controlling the activities which relate to those results. This is very noticeable in the licensed trade and leads to the highly individualistic nature of the retail outlets – the pubs – in stark contrast to the uniformity of the Marks and Spencer stores.

Methods that emphasise control over people's activities and behaviour include:

- centralisation of decision-making;
- close direct supervision/narrow span of control;
- training;
- work study, O and M and other related techniques;
- control systems based on recording of activities –

either by people entering data or automatically (tachometers, turnstiles, etc.);

- job descriptions;
- disciplinary codes;
- procedural manuals.

Those that emphasise control over results include:

- financial controls, especially budgets and variances;
- inspection/quality control;
- incentive schemes (payment by results);
- performance appraisal systems/management by objectives.

Implications for Organisation Design

The early 'classical' writers on organisation, who were concerned to develop some universal principles to guide managers, were almost exclusively concerned with control, neglecting other issues such as integration, relations with the environment and employee motivation and commitment.

Frederick Taylor (1911), for example, sought to eradicate inefficiency by increasing management control over work by breaking down complex tasks into their simple component parts, determining the most efficient way of performing each sub-task and training workers to carry out these sub-tasks in exactly the one best way. This approach combines close-direction supervision with work study and training. His approach failed to take into account the effects on employee motivation and commitment of repetitive and boring work, where the individual's contribution to the achievements of the organisation as a whole is far from clear.

Lyndall F. Urwick (1952) formulated eight principles which he felt would, if followed, lead to the design of effective organisations. With the exception of item 7, they are all about exercising control.

1 All organisations and each part of any undertaking should be the expression of a purpose, either explicit or implied – the *Principle of the Objective*.
2 Formal authority and responsibility must be coterminous and co-equal – the *Principle of Correspondence*.
3 The responsibility of higher authority for the acts of its subordinates is absolute – the *Principle of Responsibility*.
4 There must be a clear line of formal authority running from the top to the bottom of every organisation – the *Scalar Principle*.
5 No superior can supervise directly the work of more than five or, at the most, six subordinates whose work interlocks – the *Principle of the Span of Control*.
6 The work of every person in the organisation should be confined as far as possible to the performance of a single leading function – the *Principle of Specialisation*.
7 The final object of all organisation is smooth and effective co-ordination – the *Principle of Co-ordination*.
8 Every position in every organisation should be clearly prescribed in writing – the *Principle of Definition*.

An organisation designed along these lines would today be described as bureaucratic. Typically it would have a very steep hierarchy, clear statements of responsibility, detailed job descriptions and strong emphasis on functional specialisation. A high level of control over people's activities would undoubtedly be achieved, at the expense of flexibility. Organisations of this type, with elaborate arrangements for exercising control, include the banks, large retailers, and military or paramilitary organisations.

There is a tendency on the part of some modern writers on organisation – particularly academics who are accustomed to, and greatly enjoy, academic freedom – to assume that structures characterised by a high degree of central control are 'bad' while those allowing more discretion and autonomy to individuals are 'good'. It is much more useful to consider the appropriateness of different systems than to place values on them. Highly centralised control systems in which the individual is left little freedom to decide his or her own actions are quite appropriate, even essential, in some situations, while systems which leave much to the judgement of the individual are appropriate in others.

It is certainly wrong to assume that people universally react adversely to being subject to close control and supervision. Indeed some of the highest levels of employee motivation and commitment are to be found in organisations such as Marks and Spencer or the Brigade of Guards, which are characterised by high control. Also, looking at organisations from the point of view of the customer, who wants to have to wait in a supermarket queue while the check-out operator follows her own highly individual but somewhat slow method of checking groceries? In such a situation we would all vote for training in the one best method. Similarly, who would choose to fly with an airline where pre-flight checks, if any, were left to the absolute discretion of the pilot? Exercising control by monitoring results is scarcely applicable in relation to flight safety.

Summary and Conclusions

- Control has two aspects: the flow of information for control purposes; and exercising control over activities and/or outcomes.

- Both aspects need to be taken into account when designing the organisation structure.

- The starting point must be the organisation's strategy and the specific objectives to be achieved at the strategic and tactical levels.

- From these objectives performance standards should be established in respect of such areas of activity as internal efficiency and employee, customer and supplier relations.

- It will also be necessary to establish procedures for obtaining information for control purposes from sources outside the business, particularly in respect of competitors' behaviour.

- Control mechanisms – strategic milestones – need to be established to monitor the organisation's longer-term strategic development.

- The organisation structure should provide for clear, unobstructed communication channels for the timely flow of control information.

- Responsibility for generating the information must be clearly allocated.

- The imaginative use of information technology, including building a computer model of the organisation's functioning, can streamline the process and reduce unnecessary paperwork, as well as enhancing the equality of decision-making.

- Careful judgement is called for in deciding the degree of control to exercise over operations, and how to achieve the desired level of control.

- Control may be exercised directly, over activities, or indirectly, over results.

- Close, direct control is appropriate in the following circumstances:

  - when the work is capable of being clearly specified in terms of the one best way of doing it;
  - when outputs can be precisely measured as to quantity and quality;
  - when the activity involves serious risks to health and safety or risks of other kinds;
  - when close control is likely to be acceptable to or even welcomed by employees.

- In other circumstances few controls, and only indirect ones, will be appropriate, particularly in such cases as:

  - artistic or creative work;

- research;
- work which involves rapid responses to unexpected and/or unpredictable events;
- activity at the customer interface where a key customer need is flexibility of response.

- An organisation designed to achieve close control over work activities will typically have the following characteristics:

  - a steep hierarchy with relatively narrow spans of control;
  - authority is a function of level in the hierarchy;
  - a clearly defined chain of command, with clear distinctions between line management and staff in advisory or technical roles;
  - detailed job descriptions and organisation charts;
  - clearly specified performance standards covering quantity and quality of outputs;
  - specialist personnel, such as work study officers, concerned with work measurement and methods study;
  - explicit and strictly enforced rules covering such matters as punctuality, rest breaks, safety practices, etc.;
  - procedural manuals covering all standardised operations.

- Organisations where close, direct control of operations is inappropriate will typically be characterised by the following features:

  - relatively flat hierarchy with wide spans of control;

- authority located at the points in the organisation where relevant knowledge and competence are to be found;
- job content only vaguely or sketchily described;
- normally no specialist departments concerned with work measurement or methods study;
- relatively few rules or standard procedures laid down;
- more autonomous sub-units or divisions.

Two Final Thoughts

On the whole, trust is cheaper than controls.

The best way to combine information gathering with exercising influence over people's activities is called 'management by walking about'.

3

Co-ordination and Integration

The fair test of business administration, of industrial
organization is whether you have a business with all its parts
so co-ordinated, so moving together in their closely knit and
adjusting activities, so linking, interlocking, inter-relating, that
they make a working unit, not a congeries of separate
pieces.

Mary Parker Follett

Introduction

This chapter deals with two connected issues. The first,
co-ordination, is the process of ensuring that activities of
individuals or groups which are interrelated are carried
out in such a way that they complement one another and
thus make an optimum contribution to the achievement
of the objectives of the organisation as a whole. The
second – integration – refers to the ongoing and underlying process of welding the highly differentiated and
specialised parts of an organisation into a cohesive
whole.

Co-ordination

Co-ordination is called for when there is a high degree of task interdependence: in other words, in those cases where the ability of one individual, group or division to carry out a task is dependent on the way another individual, group or division carries out another, related task. There are three main types of task interdependence: sequential, reciprocal and shared resources.

Sequential interdependence exists where one person, group or division cannot perform a task until another person, group or division has performed a task occurring at an earlier stage in the production process. At department level this is exemplified by the interdependence of sales and production. At the work group or individual level it can clearly be seen in the sequence of operations on a typical assembly line.

Reciprocal interdependence exists where two or more individuals, groups or divisions must interact simultaneously in order to accomplish a task. Reciprocal interdependence between groups can be seen when, for example, two or more departments of a company have to work in very close collaboration to fulfil a particular customer contract. Reciprocal interdependence between individuals within a group can be seen any Saturday afternoon on the football field.

Interdependence due to the common use of *shared resources* exists in cases where different individuals or groups need access to a common facility – a building or a piece of equipment – to do their work, with the result that their claims on the resource, which would otherwise lead to conflict, need to be co-ordinated.

[41]

Designing Organisations

Means of Achieving Co-ordination

Co-ordination can be achieved in a variety of ways and the choice of means will have important implications for organisation design.

Co-ordination through Line Management

Where the individuals, groups or divisions needing to be co-ordinated report to the same manager, the simplest method for achieving co-ordination is to make it part of that manager's responsibilities.

Co-ordination through Staff Specialists

In many cases the activities requiring to be co-ordinated cross a number of organisational boundaries. In such cases one solution is to require co-ordination to be carried out by line management at progressively higher levels until, at the level of the chief executive, it absorbs a considerable proportion of the available time. An alternative is to set up positions or departments whose job it is to achieve co-ordination. Individual positions with this type of responsibility are variously called progress chasers, expeditors, liaison officers. Departments carry such titles as production scheduling or new product development.

Co-ordination through the Grouping of Tasks

Another obvious way of achieving co-ordination is by grouping together in divisions or departments all those activities which need to be closely co-ordinated. Most sizeable companies offering more than one product or service or operating in more than one market find the complexity of activities is such that they have to abandon a functional type of organisation structure in favour of one which groups people from different functions around a common task or purpose. This task or purpose can relate to a particular product, market or geographical area. The requirements of co-ordination will not, however, be the sole determinant of the way in which people are grouped together, and this aspect of organisation design is discussed at greater length later in this chapter.

The example of tape products manufacturing at 3M shows how improved co-ordination leads to increased efficiency. Tape is made by coating a backing with adhesive and creating a giant roll. At one time these large rolls were then taken to slitting machines in another department at the other end of the factory. The two operations had separate supervisors. Co-ordination was poor and the result was hundreds of rolls stockpiled all over the place. Quality was the responsibility of quality control inspectors and was below acceptable levels.

Now coaters and slitters work side by side. Supervision is by product line, not by function – a supervisor for all masking tape operations, for example. Quality is the responsibility of individual operatives. Inventory was cut dramatically, quality improved and manufacturing productivity increased by two-thirds.

Project Groups

Groupings for co-ordination purposes may be on a more or less permanent basis or, where the need is specific to a particular contract or to some other set of activities

[43]

bounded in time – for example making a film, launching a new product, planning and carrying out a major office relocation – they may consist of temporary task groups, variously known as project teams, task forces or working parties. It is in the nature of the activity of some industries, such as construction and civil engineering, that the work consists of a series of discrete tasks or contracts. In such instances project groups are major elements in the organisation structure.

Spontaneous or Informal Co-ordination

Many companies place great reliance on encouraging people to develop good lateral relationships and to co-ordinate their activities without reference to higher authority or any formal structural devices. In some situations this does appear to work – particularly in smaller organisations with relatively stable labour forces and where mutual interdependence is given greater emphasis by such factors as safety hazards. In the small coalfields before mechanisation, for example, face workers operated in smallish, self-selected groups known as 'marrows'. These autonomous work groups shared the financial rewards of their work and the members looked after one another in the face of common danger. In such a situation no additional measures to ensure co-ordination are needed.

Matrix Organisation

The term 'matrix management' was first used in the 1960s to describe a structure that had existed for some time in various organisations, under other names. It began to attract interest and and its use spread in the late 1960s and early 1970s since it seemed to offer a solution to some real problems. The basic structure of a matrix organisation is shown in Figure 2.

To take an example, companies in the US aerospace industry which were functionally organised were required, in order to tender for government contracts, to submit organisation charts showing that they had developed a project management system. Rather than abandon their basic functional structures the idea of positioning a set of project groups alongside a set of functional departments in a grid or matrix had strong appeal. In this context the matrix structure represents a compromise between two sets of needs: the need felt by the customer (and sometimes also by the chief executive) for clear accountability for the success of a project, and the company's need for strong specialist departments with high standards of professional or technical expertise.

In essence the matrix structure has emerged as a solution to growing complexity: the need to cope with more than one source of diversity simultaneously – different products, in different markets with different technologies. Complexity creates information overload, which can be dealt with in a number of ways: by decentralising decision-making, installing highly sophisticated computerised information systems, or creating slack resources – buffer stocks or pools of manpower. The matrix offers an alternative approach by creating lateral relationships that cut across conventional vertical lines of authority. Some enthusiasts see the matrix as the model for the organisation of the future. Others see it as an expensive, overelaborate and confusing arrangement.

[45]

Designing Organisations

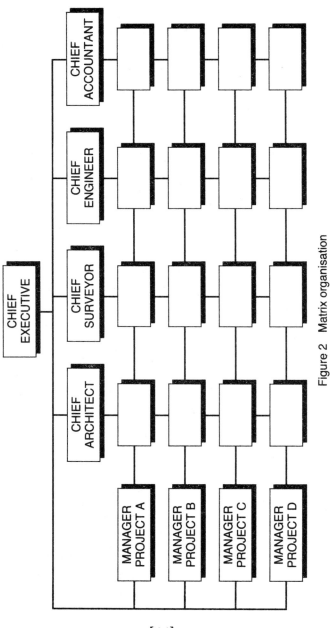

Figure 2   Matrix organisation

The enthusiasts are often attracted by the opportunities it offers to escape from the shackles of traditional hierarchical forms of organisation by working in teams in which rank and seniority count for little compared with expertise and ideas. Those who argue against it draw attention to the fact that an inescapable feature of this structure is that each person has at least two bosses and has membership in at least two groups. This can create conflict and confusion. It certainly breaks one of the golden rules of 'classical' management theory: the principle of unity of command.

In practice matrix organisations are found primarily in aerospace companies, research and development organisations, large multifunctional organisations seeking to give the same attention to products or markets as to functions, management consultants and other forms of consultancy, the construction industry, advertising agencies and business schools.

Some of the problems associated with the operation of a matrix structure are:

- Intrinsic instability – at one extreme there is a pull towards small self-contained interdisciplinary teams and at the other a pressure towards the concentration of precious functional expertise. The ensuing tug of war can eventually pull the structure in one direction or the other, while in the meantime it burns up considerable time and energy which would be better spent getting the job done.

- Unless the culture of the enterprise favours risk-taking, decisions are pushed up the structure until a cross-over point is reached where authority clearly resides. This can delay and distort decision-making.

[47]

- Individuals often experience difficulty in handling the ambiguity and uncertainty about such things as role, status and authority.

Kenneth Knight (1977) sums up the pros and cons of matrix management excellently, using the criteria of efficiency, control and accountability, co-ordination, adaptation and 'social effectiveness'. He concludes that matrix structures can maintain or increase efficiency in cases where key resources are distributed among sub-units, but that the introduction of matrix structures into very rigid formal organisations can actually reduce efficiency.

Control and accountability can be readily achieved by organisations using matrix structures, in respect of both the efficient use of resources and the accomplishment of task objectives. Co-ordination is achieved through matrix structures, but expensively so, and such structures are, therefore, justified only in situations where there is a high degree of interdependence against tight deadlines and strict technical or other specifications. Adaptation is facilitated by the matrix organisation through its ability to facilitate the rapid exchange of information and ideas actually and diagonally through the structure. Social effectiveness is limited since matrix structures tend to generate stress, confusion and conflict.

Co-ordination by Committee

This is probably the least effective means of achieving co-ordination between different groups within the same organisation. The weaknesses of committees are well known, and include the following.

- Members attend as representatives of their departments or functions. Their minds are set less on achieving smooth co-operation than on protecting departmental interests or competing for resources.

- Committee effectiveness is lowered by failings in chairmanship. In particular, where the chairman is drawn from one of the activity areas to be co-ordinated he or she can be open to the charge of bias; weak chairmanship can lead to time wasting and poor-quality decision-making.

- Committees have proved to be notoriously uneconomic when their outputs are measured against the hours involved in them.

- Committees tend to compromise between conflicting interests rather than make optimal decisions, or accept risks. They involve the very real danger of 'group-think'.

- Getting the right people together for meetings is difficult, with the result that meetings are subject to cancellation or are spaced apart. This inevitably slows decision-making.

Implications for Organisation Design

Bearing in mind that the requirements of co-ordination cannot be treated in isolation from the other objectives of the design process, the following procedure is suggested.

- Identify those activities which do need to be closely co-ordinated and consider the advantages and

[49]

disadvantages of grouping them into organisational units.

- Where such activities *are* grouped into single organisational units, select appropriate processes for ensuring co-ordination takes place:
  - making line management responsible;
  - creating specialist staff for the purpose;
  - encouraging informal, spontaneous co-operation.

- Where co-ordination *between* groups continues to be required, select the appropriate processes for achieving it:
  - making higher-level line management responsible;
  - creating project groups or task forces;
  - appointing liaison officers;
  - creating specialist staff;
  - creating a matrix structure.

- Whereas committees can be useful for certain purposes (such as health and safety), seriously consider abolishing all committees that have been set up to achieve co-ordination between departments – it is highly probable that they are not cost effective.

Co-ordination at Corporate Level

The objectives of co-ordination at corporate level include:

- ensuring that different parts of the organisation are contributing to its objectives as a whole;

- achieving economies in the use of resources, for example through common purchasing policies;

- ensuring the supply of future top management for the corporation through the co-ordination of 'fast-track' management development programmes;

- resolving conflicting claims on capital for investment programmes;

- agreeing transfer prices where appropriate.

The difficulty and the cost of achieving co-ordination grow in proportion to the increase in diversity of the activities requiring to be co-ordinated. The main ones are functions, products and markets.

Functions

At the simplest level, in the small firm led by an entrepreneur and having a single product, the sole requirement is to co-ordinate functions – principally manufacturing operations and sales. As the firm grows in size, while remaining essentially a single-product company, the range of important functions will grow and the need for co-ordination at corporate level may also embrace finance, personnel, engineering, computing, research and development and others. A typical functional structure is illustrated in Figure 3.

Products

The problem of co-ordination becomes more complex as additional product lines are added and specialised sub-units of the organisation, such as manufacturing plants,

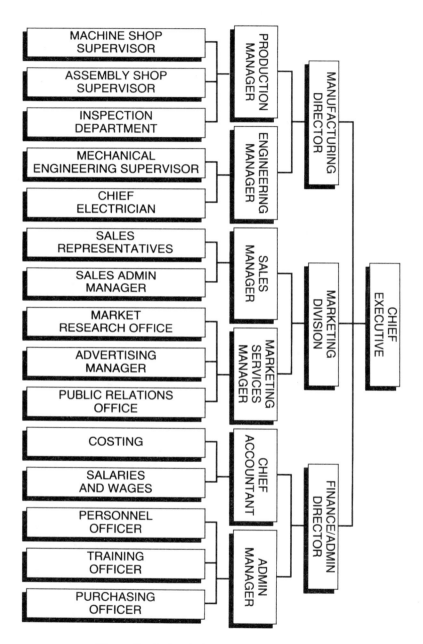

Figure 3   A simple functional organisation

assembly lines, salesforces or product development teams, are created around these new products. The nature of the co-ordination problem varies considerably, however, according to the nature of product diversity. In some instances, typified by oil companies, there is a *dominant* product (oil) and a series of related 'downstream' products – petroleum, propane gas, chemical feedstocks, agricultural products, etc. – which reflect diverse applications of a basic technology. In such organisations the need for functional co-ordination also remains high.

At the other extreme the products may be quite unrelated. For example, the Hanson Trust has a portfolio which includes a large range of unrelated products and until recently BAT covered tobacco, paper, retailing and insurance. In such cases there is little need or scope for co-ordination and the degree to which it is exercised is really a matter of philosophy or style. At one extreme, as Goold and Campbell (1987) point out, the holding company approach adopted by companies such as Hanson and BTR limits itself to the exercise of financial control. In other cases, however, co-ordination of strategic plans, management development and purchasing policies (in respect of computers, for example) may be attempted. BP exemplifies this approach. In between is the grey area of *related* products – typified by ICI, where the products are sufficiently differentiated so that no single product dominates yet are linked by a common technology: chemicals. In these cases there is a strong need for co-ordination of activities which focus on products since interdependence is usually considerable and product-based divisionalisation is perhaps the most commonly encountered form of organisation – certainly among companies operating in a single national geographical market. Figure 4 shows a structure based on product divisions.

Markets

Differentiation by market can take various forms. In some cases each market calls for products significantly different from those required by other markets; the problem of co-ordination is then essentially an extension of product group co-ordination. An example would be a company supplying toiletries to the consumer market and pharmaceutical products to the medical profession and/or health services industry. Such an organisation would normally achieve co-ordination of activities through a toiletries division and a pharmaceuticals division.

A quite different case exists where the product is essentially the same but needs to be adapted or modified to meet the requirements of particular market segments. This applies in the case of computers, for example, which require special hardware and software modifications to meet the special needs of government, banking, the airline industry, telecommunications and other sectors. Such cases would need specialised sub-units concentrating on market segments as well as others focusing on products, thus intensifying the amount of co-ordination required. A market-based structure is illustrated in Figure 5.

Geographical markets

As company activities develop across international frontiers yet further structural differentiation is needed,

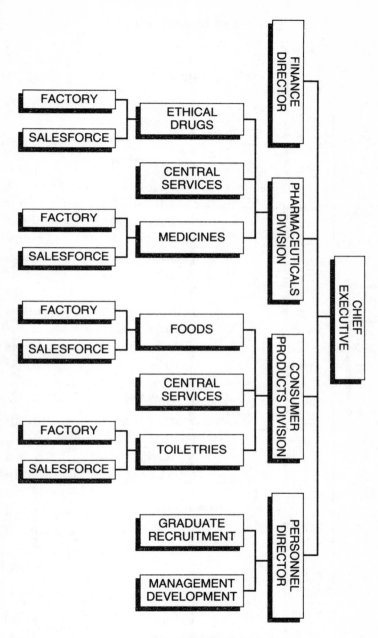

Figure 4   Product divisionalisation

[55]

Designing Organisations

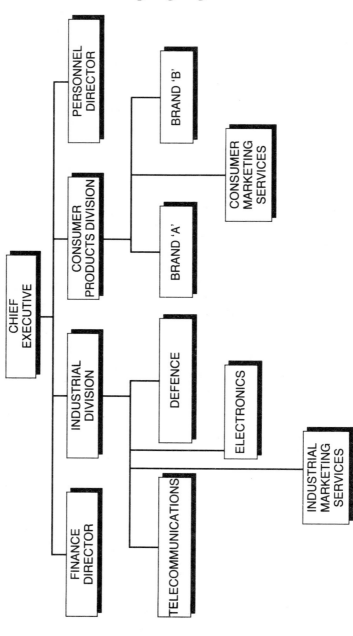

Figure 5   Market divisionalisation

[56]

to reflect the need for specialised sub-units located in and focusing on different geographical markets. Figure 6 is an example of this type of structure.

The International Company

The peak of differentiation and hence the most complex co-ordination task of all occurs in the large international company which:

- operates with highly complex technology calling for highly specialised functional expertise;

- has a wide range of *related* products such that interdependence between them is high;

- operates with these products in different markets which demand special product adaptations;

- operates in a wide range of countries with different political systems, stages of economic development and national cultures.

Figure 7 provides an example of an organisation with a structure designed to cope simultaneously with several types of differentiation.

What Companies Do in Practice

John Daniels and colleagues (1985) studied the organisation structures of thirty-seven US companies with both high product diversity and high dependence on foreign sales. The researchers set up a number of hypotheses and tested them.

[57]

Designing Organisations

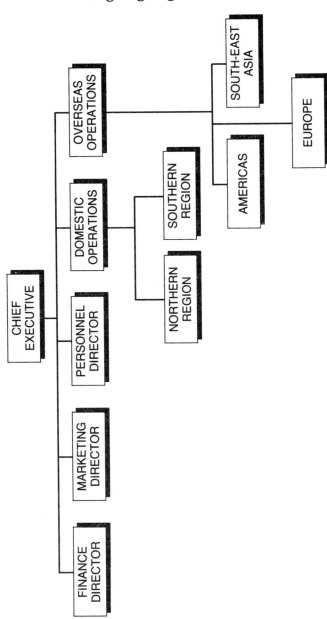

Figure 6   Regional Divisionalisation

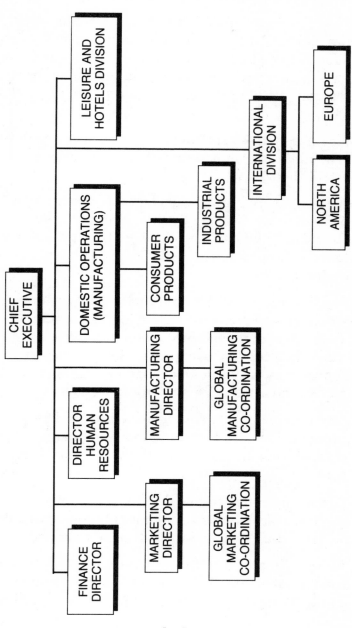

Figure 7 Complex divisionalisation

Designing Organisations

- Few if any firms handle foreign operations through functional structures. *Outcome*: only two firms used a functional structure, but these were oil companies, having many products but being vertically integrated and essentially based on a single product – oil.

- Few use matrix structures. *Outcome*: only one did so. (The unity of command principle is perhaps too well established.)

- As complexity grows, global *product* structures will be found more frequently than international division structures. *Outcome*: true if diversity of products is looked at, but not true if the criterion is dependence on foreign sales.

- Some firms will stick to international division structures despite very high levels of product diversity and dependence on foreign sales. *Outcome*: true. They cope by using other devices such as committees, task forces, changed rewards systems and strong articulation of corporate goals.

- Conglomerates (i.e. companies with unrelated products) use product divisions more than companies with related products. *Outcome*: very true.

- Firms with international division structures invest more in research and development than companies with product structures. *Outcome*: not verified.

- Firms with area division structures depend more on foreign sales than firms with either international or product division structures. *Outcome*: not significant.

Sheppard and Wells's (1972) study of the organisation structures of 187 large US-based companies operating worldwide concluded that corporations facing international expansion typically adopt different organisation structures at different stages in the process. They, too, selected two variables as measures of growing complexity: foreign sales as a percentage of total sales, and the number of different products sold internationally.

In the early stages companies usually manage international operations through an international division. Subsequently, companies with limited product diversity typically adopt an area structure while companies with considerable product diversity and a high volume of foreign sales adopt a matrix structure.

Although the global matrix appeared to offer the perfect solution, for many companies the result was disappointing: 'the promised land of the global matrix turned out to be an organizational quagmire from which they were forced to retreat'.

Dow Chemical, one of the companies to pioneer the global matrix, eventually returned to a more conventional structure with clear lines of responsibility assigned to area managers. Citibank also abandoned the matrix after experimenting with it for several years. The main difficulties encountered were: decision processes which were slow, costly and acrimonious; and energy was sapped by constant travelling and frequent meetings.

Bartlett and Ghoshal (1989) quote one senior executive among those they interviewed who perceptively said that the problem was not so much how to change the organisation structure into a matrix but how to create a matrix in the minds of managers.

[61]

Designing Organisations

The Case of Procter & Gamble

Bartlett and Ghoshal provide an interesting account of the evolution of structure in Procter & Gamble.

Until the 1950s the structure was a simple *functional* one, with the marketing function dominant. Sales were concentrated in the USA. Overseas operations were relatively small and confined to the UK and Canada. In 1955 the domestic operation was divisionalised by *product* – detergents, personal products and food products. In the late 1950s, as international growth occurred, the international side was structured around *geographical* markets. The *functional* influence on local companies remained strong, particularly in marketing, where brand management, extensive market research and product testing were universally imposed practices. There was, however, no strong integration of product strategies.

In the 1970s problems were caused by rising raw materials costs, checks to the growth of consumer spending and intensified competition. The need for a more co-ordinated *product* strategy was felt. In the late 1970s the company strengthened its European research and development facility and organised it along *product* lines. 'Euro-teams' were established to achieve new product development on a Europe-wide basis. The results included such famous brands as Ariel soap powder, Fairy dishwashing liquid and Camay soap. Subsequently, 'Euro-brand teams' were developed comprising brand and advertising managers from local subsidiaries and key functional managers from head office, led by the general manager of the subsidiary chosen to be the lead company for that particular brand.

In the 1980s, as product innovation became an increasingly important competitive weapon in global markets, research and development in the USA was also strengthened and reorganised into *product streams*.

Integration

Integration is the process of binding together the various parts of an organisation into a cohesive whole. It is a more general, more diffused process than co-ordination, which relates to specific identifiable task interdependencies. It has more to do with states of mind and attitudes than with concrete activities and behaviours.

By definition, integration is the process of bringing together individuals or groups who have been differentiated or separated in some way. The most common organisational boundaries that pull people apart from one another and distract them from focusing on the goals of the organisation as a whole are:

- functional boundaries, between different specialisations or between line and staff;
- geographical boundaries, between staff in different locations;
- hierarchical boundaries – especially those between staff paid monthly (white collar workers) and employees paid weekly (blue collar workers), and between people in head office and those in operating divisions and subsidiaries;
- historically derived boundaries – usually following mergers, separating people according to which party

to the merger or acquisition they originally belonged to. (In the British confectionery/soft drinks business Cadbury Schweppes, for example, there is still a clearly visible boundary between Cadbury and Schweppes staff after twenty years.)

Approaches to integration can include:

- Abolish the boundaries.

  - As far as possible, group together people from different functions in multidisciplinary teams, either permanently or in project groups or matrix structures.
  - Move as rapidly as possible towards single status by abolishing all the traditional – and operationally unnecessary – class and status distinctions between blue and white collar workers. Make everyone a salaried employee, paid monthly. Lay down the same hours of work and conditions of employment (sickness pay, pensions, etc.) for everyone. Do away with separate lunch facilities, toilets or entrances. (In the context of British society this will not be easy or capable of being achieved overnight. Expect as much resistance from blue collar employees as from those in white collar jobs. It *can* be done in Britain, however, as companies like IBM and Sony have demonstrated.)

- Move people backwards and forwards freely across the boundaries that cannot be broken down. Encourage social interaction, sports events and other opportunities to meet and mix.

[64]

- Use training programmes, at all levels from induction courses to top management seminars, to reinforce a feeling of identification with the firm.

- Link people throughout the organisation by the emotional and psychological bonds of a strong corporate culture. (This is a subject in itself and is dealt with in Chapter 7.)

Summary

- All organisations involve ways of breaking down overall tasks into smaller elements and then tying them together again.

- This tying together involves two related processes: co-ordination of specific activities, and integration at the emotional and attitudinal level.

- Co-ordination can be achieved in the following ways:

  - through line management;
  - through staff specialists;
  - grouping interdependent activities together;
  - encouraging spontaneous co-ordination;
  - by means of a matrix structure.

  It is unlikely that committees can be effective in achieving co-ordination.

- Co-ordination at corporate level involves difficult organisational problems as size and diversity

[65]

increase and operations become more complex. Companies can be structured by function, product, market segment or geographical area.

- Integration is the process of binding together the various parts of the organisation into a cohesive whole. It can be achieved by such means as abolishing boundaries or distinctions between groups of employees, mobility of personnel, social interaction, training and by building a strong corporate culture.

4

Organisation and Environment

Introduction

Organisations are clearly not self-contained entities. They achieve their purposes by engaging in transactions of various kinds with the outside world. They import capital from shareholders, labour from the community, materials, equipment and services of all kinds from other organisations in the public and private sectors. In return they export goods and services. These activities are continuously subject to constraints arising from the actions of other organisations with which they may have no direct links: competitors, government departments, trade unions in other industries, the press and many others. Finally, the organisation is embedded in a national and international environmental context and its destiny is influenced by political, economic and social changes quite outside its control.

There are, therefore, three distinct levels of environmental interaction which need to be taken into account in the process of organisation design.

- The immediate (or 'transactional') environment, which relates to inputs and outputs – primarily consisting of customers and suppliers.

Designing Organisations

- The intermediate (or 'constraining') environment, which exercises strong and short- to medium-term influences on the organisation – pressure groups, trade unions, planning authorities and various governmental agencies.

- The general (or 'contextual') environment, which also powerfully influences the organisation's ability to achieve its objectives but with greater emphasis on the medium to longer term, made up of a wide range of political, social, economic and technological factors.

From the point of view of the design process there are two main tasks: designing the organisation in such a way as, first, *to provide a good fit with its transactional and constraining environments* (this issue is dealt with later in this chapter); and, second, *to be flexible and responsive to the need to change* resulting from trends, events and changes in the *constraining* and *contextual* environments (discussed in Chapter 6).

The implications for organisation design will reflect the particular circumstances of each individual organisation's strategic and operational objectives and the relative importance of the different components of the transactional environment. For example, in one set of circumstances – say, food retailing in supermarkets – winning market share may be the most critical factor leading to success. If so, the organisation must be designed in such a way that power and authority reside with those roles and groups most likely to be able to influence customer behaviour and preferences. In other circumstances the critical transactions may be to do with trade union negotiations or the ability to recruit highly qualified personnel, to secure supplies of scarce materials or energy, to acquire sites or premises in strategic locations or to raise capital in financial markets.

What does it mean, to adapt the organisation structure to fit the environment in which the business is operating? It means having a structure which achieves the following objectives.

- Transactions with the environment are under control in the same way that internal operations are. For example, supplies of the right quality are being purchased at the best price; customer satisfaction is at the high level specified in corporate marketing objectives.

- Transactions with the environment are well co-ordinated. For example, although it may make sense for more than one sales representative from the same organisation to call on a single potential client, their calls should be made with the other's full knowledge and their objectives should not overlap.

- Personnel in contact with individuals and organisations in the environment are the ambassadors of the organisation; not only in dealings with customers but with community representatives, potential recruits to the organisation and government officials. It is particularly important that they are committed to the organisation and its goals, and are seen to be so.

- As the environment changes, so the structure needs to be flexible and capable of adapting to a new situation.

Structural Alignment with the Transactional Environment

The basic structural alignment of an organisation has been discussed in the previous chapter. Organisations structured primarily around markets or market segments or geographical areas are most likely to provide a good fit with the transactional environment. Organisations with product divisions may also provide a good fit in cases where there is a close match between a particular product and a clearly defined market segment. When the products are all different but aimed at the same target group of customers, however, the market focus can be lost and a production orientation can develop.

Market segment divisionalisation gives greater and more explicit emphasis to the critical importance of the market and the customer. The major divisions are built around types of customer – for example, in the electronics field the range of customers for microprocessors could consist of government departments, consumer electronics goods manufacturers, the telecommunications industry and manufacturers of automation and industrial control equipment. (This type of structure provides an elegant solution where there is just one basic product but can become messy when the product range is very wide.)

Geographical area divisionalisation is another form of market-related structure, in which the major divisions are regions of the world, national markets or regional markets within a country. This structure is most commonly found where there are major geographical differences in trading conditions calling for specialised knowledge and where the nature of the organisation's activities is such that the product or service must be produced as well as marketed locally.

Bartlett and Ghoshal (1989) use Unilever as an example of an organisation with a structure largely determined by variations in market conditions. In laundry detergents there is little scope for standardising products in Europe, let alone globally. As late as 1980 washing machine penetration ranged from less than 30 per cent of households in the UK to over 85 per cent in Germany. In northern European countries people boiled their dirty clothes whereas in Mediterranean countries there was still considerable attachment to hand washing in cold water. Differences in water hardness, perfume preferences, fabric mix and phosphate legislation made product differentiation between countries essential. It was also necessary to take the structure of national markets into account. In 1985 five retail chains controlled 65 per cent of the German market while the Italian market was highly fragmented. Different countries had different laws governing advertising and the use of various forms of sales promotion. The manufacturing operations were capable of being carried on efficiently on a relatively small scale so that it was economic in all but the smallest countries to produce close to the market.

Unilever's structural solution – to build strong local companies, sensitive to local conditions and allowing them freedom of action with minimum interference from the centre – worked well in the circumstances. Less effective solutions were those of Kao and Procter & Gamble. Kao competed primarily on the basis of having very efficient central plants and centralised research and development. It approached the world as if it were a

[71]

single undifferentiated market in an attempt to exploit the economies associated with standard products, centralised global manufacturing and high controls from the centre. Procter & Gamble adopted the middle path, by developing new products in the USA and transferring them abroad, backed by a powerful expertise in marketing, with local manufacture and some degree of decentralisation of control. The company ran into considerable initial difficulties, however, when it tried to introduce Tide and other successful US brands into other countries.

Representational or Boundary Roles

Some organisational roles are vested with the authority to act on the organisation's behalf. The action may involve entering into contracts to buy or sell, hiring employees, communicating with the media, lobbying politicians or negotiating with trade unions.

The requirements for filling such roles will vary according to the nature and degree of professional expertise or skill involved and the extent to which the actions are critical for organisational success. Negotiating an annual wage agreement with a major trade union will call for a high level of knowledge and skill and the outcome could be of vital importance for the company. In consequence the selection of the right person to fill the role will be particularly important. The rewards and status associated with such a post will normally be among the highest in the enterprise. It can be a critical factor in the success or otherwise of the negotiations that the occupant of the role is given a free hand – that is to say that full delegation of responsibility and authority is given.

On the other hand, hiring unskilled temporary labourers will not demand a high level of skill nor will the outcome critically affect the organisation's success. This task can be delegated to first-line supervision and the extent to which they will be required to follow strictly laid-down procedures or are expected to exercise their own discretion is a matter for debate and choice.

Taking the market/customer aspect of the environment as an example, the range of such boundary roles in organisations of any size is considerable:

- *Marketing* – marketing director, marketing manager and marketing assistant; advertising manager, brand manager, market research officer and account executive.

- *Sales/customers* – sales director, sales manager and sales representative; customer service manager and customer service operative; sales administration manager and sales clerk.

The effectiveness of these various roles will largely reflect their positioning in the structure in terms of authority and status, the level of care taken in their selection and the extent to which they are highly trained and professional in their specialised fields. Where a particular customer relationship is vital to the success of the organisation the boundary role may be assumed by the chief executive or chairman – as when negotiating a government contract at ministerial level. As a general rule, the status and authority of the person in the boundary role should match the status and authority of the customer's representative.

Typical 'boundary' roles outside the sales and marketing functions include: industrial relations manager, public relations officer, community relations officer, recruitment officer, buyer and investor relations manager.

Those whose work requires them to specialise in boundary roles and to relate the organisation to the outside world often face conflicts in carrying out these roles since their day-to-day working relationships bring them more frequently into contact with 'outsiders' than with members of their own organisations. As Miller and Rice (1967) have pointed out, the tendency is for such people to identify themselves more with the individuals with whom they do business daily than with the parent organisation. In a case they describe, sales staff in a dry cleaning company identified themselves with their customers to an extent that prejudiced the company's interests. Pressures of a similar nature are also often present in the buying role or that of the full-time industrial relations negotiator. This is a difficult problem for the organisation to handle, since in many ways the establishment of links with the environment through personal relationships can be beneficial to it. Many organisations tend to tackle it in the wrong way – by imposing a level of control on those engaged in boundary roles which is inappropriate to the nature of the task. A more effective approach is to take steps to ensure that those performing boundary roles are highly committed to the organisation. One way to achieve this is to endeavour to make these roles as satisfying as possible – which implies minimising rather than maximising controls. This strategy must, however, be supported by the steps taken to integrate boundary activities with the rest of the organisation.

The problem of integration of boundary roles can be exemplified by examining the sales representative's role and the problems involved in integrating it with internal roles, particularly in the production area. In the worst case, the sales and production functions are completely separated – socially as well as geographically. The sales staff become completely identified with the customers and with satisfying their needs, regardless of the benefit to the organisation of so doing, while production staff become totally immersed in their own technical problems and processes. Such a state of affairs can be avoided by a combination of the following strategies:

- the creation of frequent opportunities for face-to-face contacts between sales and production personnel;

- exchange of personnel between the salesforce and production departments;

- a basic organisation structure that emphasises market segment or territory rather than function;

- a status system which does not generate significant inequalities – and hence barriers to integration – between internal and boundary roles;

- 'Customer care' training for product personnel.

Vertical Integration

This approach to dealing with pressures in the transactional environment involves either reaching back into the input chain and securing essential supplies by integrating supplying organisations into the host organisation or reaching forward into the output chain and acquiring organisations that are actual or potential distributors or consumers of the host company's products. Swedish timber-producing companies, for example, own paper mills and converting plants producing packaging materials in many countries. Boots, essentially a retailer, manufactures many of the products to be found in its chain of stores.

The advantages and disadvantages of vertical integration have been studied by economists and the whole subject is too complex to explore fully here. Some key points can, however, be made.

A valid strategic reason for vertical integration will exist at a given point in time if the alternative is to be starved of inputs or blocked as far as distribution channels or other outlets for the product are concerned. Circumstances change over time, however, and many companies retain a degree of vertical integration long after it has ceased to carry any strategic advantages.

Vertical integration involves internal transfer pricing and dampens the impact of market forces on a company's activities. In such conditions it becomes very difficult to measure efficiency and competitiveness objectively.

An organisational strategy which falls short of vertical integration yet which can ensure continuity and quality of supplies is the approach taken by Marks and Spencer in the UK towards its suppliers. The giant retailer acts as guarantor, banker, efficiency consultant and trainer in respect of its key suppliers and binds them to it in a very close relationship, which nevertheless falls short of acquisition.

Marks and Spencer has been described as a manufacturer without factories working with manufacturers who are retailers without stores. The company analyses the requirements of its customers, and transmits them rapidly to its suppliers. It employs large numbers of technical advisers who help suppliers improve productivity and raise quality. It exercises the strictest quality control and also specifies and controls not only the raw materials used but also the packaging.

Marks and Spencer suppliers were largely shielded from the effects of the major recession in the early 1980s. Whereas 26,000 jobs were lost in the clothing industry in 1981 and twenty-eight plants closed in the first half of 1982, Marks and Spencer suppliers – such as the Leicester knitwear firm Corah, the suit manufacturers Dewhirst and Freddie Miller – all flourished. Corah supplies 60 per cent of its output to Marks and Spencer, the other companies 90 per cent.

Subcontracting

Boundary activities of organisations are sometimes subcontracted. Selling, for example, is frequently subcontracted to agents, especially in overseas territories; it is common practice to employ agencies for advertising, market research, public relations and recruiting, and consultants to develop marketing strategies; after-sales service is also frequently sub-contracted to specialist firms.

Alternatively – although this is less frequently encountered – the process is turned upside down in that the company concentrates on marketing and selling a product and subcontracts the manufacturing. An example is the small short-haul aircraft, the Brittan–Norman Islander, which is manufactured by subcontractors in Romania.

Smaller enterprises can seldom afford to employ a full range of specialists of high calibre across the whole range of boundary roles, so that using subcontractors makes sound sense. It is vitally important, however, that the subcontractors become reasonably closely integrated with the host company and understand its activities and culture at a deep level.

The Organisation of the Marketing Function

The task of the marketing function of a business is to manage the relationship between the business and its market(s) in such a way that the long-term profitability and survival of the enterprise are assured. This will certainly involve selling goods or services to customers at prices that ensure an adequate return on investment. It will, however, involve much more than this – a dynamic process carried on in the context of environmental change, which matches competence possessed by the organisation to needs, both existing and potential, in the market.

Organisation structures in the marketing function of business enterprises appear to vary in five main respects:

- the extent to which marketing activities are clearly differentiated from other activities;

- the way in which marketing activities are grouped into organisational units;

- the extent to which there is task specialisation within the marketing function;

- configuration, i.e. number of levels in the hierarchy; spans of control;

- the arrangements for managing the interface with the market.

Differentiation of the Marketing Function

In smaller enterprises marketing may form part of the responsibilities of the chief executive and in such cases no clearly defined marketing function will exist as part of the formal organisation structure. Larger organisations having just a single product normally do have a separate marketing function established as a department of the company headed up by a marketing director (if the company takes marketing seriously) or a marketing manager.

In cases where a company has more than one product or serves several distinct markets the situation is more complex. Where the divisional structure consists of product divisions the organisation choices are:

[79]

- each product division has it own marketing department;

- there is a central marketing division servicing the needs of all the product divisions;

- each product division has its own marketing department but the activities of these departments are co-ordinated by a central marketing division.

Where the structure is chiefly based on market divisions, e.g. industrial market, consumer market, government market, by definition each division has its own marketing organisation. There is still a choice, however, whether or not to have a corporate-level marketing function exercising co-ordination and carrying out such tasks as corporate advertising.

These choices cannot be made in isolation but have to be made alongside decisions about the other choices to be outlined below.

The Way in which the Marketing Activities are Grouped into Organisation Units

Where are the internal organisational boundaries to be drawn which will differentiate one marketing specialism from another? Marketing specialists may be grouped into teams by type of product, by brand, by market segment being served or by geographical area. In large complex organisations all three forms of grouping may be required. Much depends in practice on decisions previously taken about the basic structure of the organisation as a whole. For example, if the basic structure involves product divisions it is sensible to organise the marketing function within each product division on the basis of the particular brands, market segments or geographical areas. If there is, in addition, a corporate level marketing function this is most likely to be effective if based on grouping by market, with the marketing function within product divisions being differentiated on the basis of brands or geographical areas.

Degree of Specialisation of Marketing Tasks

The range of specialised tasks and related job titles in the marketing/sales area is considerable. The list below is by no means exhaustive.

Marketing	*Sales*
Marketing manager	Sales manager
Marketing services manager	Sales representative/agent
Market research manager	Sales administration manager
Consumer research manager	Sales clerk
Customer relations manager	After-sales service manager
Complaints manager	Advertising manager
Business development manager	Public relations officer
Account executive	Press relations officer
Brand manager	Estimator

When designing the marketing organisation two quite different approaches can be adopted. One is to focus on products, markets or brands and to require individuals or small teams to handle all or most of the marketing and sales tasks listed above. The opposite approach is to build strong task specialisation and to require specialists to spread their activities across several markets, products or brands.

The key to the appropriate form of structure lies in the

[81]

extent to which highly specialised knowledge of particular markets, products or brands is critical to success. Where products are standardised and technologically simple, markets are relatively unsophisticated and brands well established in the market, the focus of specialisation should be the particular expertise associated with the different tasks of selling, market research, advertising and so on. Where, however, the products are complex, markets are highly sophisticated and new brands are being launched, it may be more productive to focus on the common objective and risk dilution of functional expertise.

Configuration

A. K. Rice (1958) points out that the introduction of extra but unnecessary levels in the management hierarchy is perhaps best illustrated in large consumer salesforces, in which salesmen report to field sales managers, who report to branch managers, who report to district managers, who report to regional managers, who report to divisional managers, who report to the general sales manager – who reports to the sales director. He found six-level hierarchies to be not uncommon and five levels usual. For such a structure to be sensible there would need to be significant differences in the nature of the job at each level – field territory, branch and district, etc. Although such differences may exist at regional level – say between the north of England and the south – or at divisional level, between one product group and another, they are most unlikely to exist at lower levels. Rice conjures up a ridiculous picture (using the models of Ford motor cars in vogue in the 1960s) of the representative in his Anglia being followed by the field sales manager in his Consul and the branch manager in his Zephyr – and so on up the hierarchy until the procession is completed by the sales director in his Bentley. He argues that the workload on representatives stems more from their own 'towering hierarchies than from the pressures of customers and competitors'.

Interface with the Market

Organisations can be divided in a rough and ready way into two groups. In one are those which deal directly with customers. In doing so they may use all or any of a number of interface modes, including:

- own retail outlets, e.g. The Body Shop, Clarks Shoes, Thomson Holidays (Lunn Poly);

- direct salesforce calling on customers, e.g. suppliers of office equipment and stationery, printers, insurance salespersons;

- mail order, e.g. 'direct from manufacturer' clothing companies;

- speciality selling, e.g. Tupperware parties.

In the other group are those which deal with the final customer only through intermediaries: agents, dealers, distributors, wholesalers, retailers.

There are, of course, many organisations which use both approaches to the market. Clearly there are considerable implications for structure whichever approach is adopted.

In some instances, the organisation has little or no choice as to the form of distribution channel it employs. It would be difficult to sell Mars bars direct to the public, bypassing confectionary shops and supermarkets, or steel direct to industry, bypassing stockholders. The interesting cases from the viewpoint of organisation design are those where there is a choice. Why is Tupperware not available in shops? Why can you buy Avon cosmetics only from the Avon Lady? Why does Guinness stand alone among brewers and not own its own retail outlets? Why do some clothing companies sell direct to the public rather than through the retail trade?

Creating a Market Orientation – Organisations where 'the Customer is King'

For organisations where the interface with the market and/or the customer is the most important aspect of its interaction with the transactional environment (and most business organisations fall into this category) it is not enough to structure the company in alignment with its markets or create boundary roles. There is a need beyond this: to educate every member of the organisation in the importance of responsiveness to the market and customer service. Ways in which this can be done are dealt with in some detail in Chapter 7. There are, however, some structural devices that can be employed to reinforce cultural values and norms. In Lloyds Bank, for example, customer service teams have been formed in many branches, involving staff who do not normally interact greatly with customers in the process of generating ideas to improve custom service. In Scandinavian Airlines and several other market-oriented companies the organisation chart has been turned upside down, along the lines indicated in Figure 8, in order to stress that authority ultimately stems from the market place.

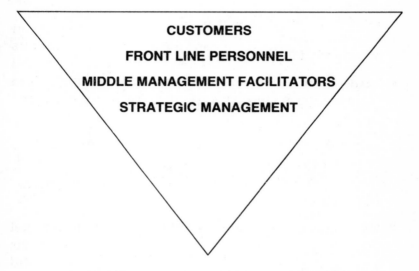

CUSTOMERS

FRONT LINE PERSONNEL

MIDDLE MANAGEMENT FACILITATORS

STRATEGIC MANAGEMENT

Figure 8   The inverted, market-oriented organisation chart

Summary

In designing an organisation careful consideration needs to be given to ensuring a good fit with other organisations and individuals in its *transactional* and *constraining* environments – those individuals or organisations which supply inputs or consume outputs or whose actions significantly influence the outcome of the organisation's activities.

The tools available for ensuring such a good fit include:

- structural alignment with the environment – chiefly with the market, by means of divisionalisation based on market segments, geographical areas or, where appropriate, products;
- boundary roles – positions in the organisation structure which focus on relationships with suppliers of inputs or outputs;
- vertical integration – the strategic process of securing inputs or distribution channels for outputs by acquisition;
- subcontracting – particularly in cases where the organisation cannot afford to employ full time the range of expertise required to handle relations with transactional parties;
- the organisation of the marketing function itself:
  - the extent to which it is differentiated;
  - the way in which marketing tasks are grouped together;
  - the degree of task specialisation within the marketing function;
  - the configuration of the marketing organisation;
  - the nature of the interface with the market;
- creating a market-oriented organisation – this is mainly a function of corporate culture but structural devices such as customer service teams drawn from personnel other than those in boundary roles can help.

5

Designing Organisations for Motivation and Commitment

Introduction

According to Roy Thornton, plant manager with Procter & Gamble, 'Americans will one day thank the Japanese for waking us up'. His plant in Greensboro, North Carolina, manufactures hair-care products, dentifrice and deodorants. Its 500 employees are grouped into teams of ten to twelve and every day each team meets for thirty minutes (in company time) in its own meeting room, to plan and co-ordinate its activities. As well as being responsible for a clearly defined business function, such as manufacturing, packaging or distributing a particular brand of product, the team also allocates its members to share in plant-wide tasks such as maintenance, cleaning and even office work. 'Here there is no such thing as an accountant.' Employee involvement is not, however, restricted to the organisation and execution of everyday tasks. It begins at the strategic level, focusing on how to out-perform Procter & Gamble's major competitors: not just the traditional ones – Colgate and Unilever – but the future threat from Japan in the shape of Kao. Information about strategy, tactics, profits and market share is fully disclosed. When Thornton embarked on his radical approach to running the factory he was not allowed to give certain information to the shop floor on the grounds that it might leak through to the competition. So he used his initiative and obtained the information from Nielsen – the market research agency – thus demonstrating that the material was already in the public domain. This degree of openness has now been adopted throughout the company. Strategic issues are debated annually; the plant is shut down and everybody attends a strategic workshop in which the corporate vice-presidents participate.

Thornton believes strongly in the importance of innovation and argues that it springs from the creativity of people of all kinds and at all levels – 'God didn't just make managers the creative ones.' He taps worker creativity in two ways: first through the work teams described above and, second, through 'diagonal slice' groups each consisting of a cross-section of employees – men and women, blacks and whites. These groups designed the production and pay systems, and take decisions about manning and recruiting. Thornton accepts their decisions provided they do not violate the 'Greensboro Principles' – a set of values developed in discussion with employers and printed on a plastic card carried by every employee. The key values are:

- high standards of performance;
- winning through teamwork;
- being an owner – managing the business, through the team, as though each individual were using his or her own personal resources;

- treating each employee as an individual;
- honesty and integrity;
- good communication;
- a safe, clean, healthy working environment;
- employment stability through building a successful business.

The shared values are given further expression through a list of 'golden threads' which bind the members of the organisation together. These are printed on the reverse side of the same plastic card:

- safety;
- high quality;
- low cost;
- customer service;
- a multicultural organisation effectively using the abilities of peoples of both sexes and all races;
- timely information;
- high appearance standards.

Most organisations are designed primarily to facilitate the control and co-ordination of the activities of one group of people (the employees) by another group of people (the managers). Designs having these objectives reflect a number of assumptions. The first and most obvious is that managers know best; the second that employees are not to be trusted; the third that controlling what people do with their hands and feet is more important than winning their hearts and minds.

Some of the most spectacularly successful organisations in the modern world have been designed on the basis of an entirely different philosophy – one based on the view that employee motivation and commitment is the most powerful competitive weapon of all. Procter & Gamble's Greensboro plant is one of a growing number of organisations representing this approach.

Many of the ideas being built into radical approaches to organisation design in North America and Western Europe have been modelled on or adapted from Japanese management practice – in particular such things as quality circles and an egalitarian approach to working conditions. Above all, Japanese industry's success in the sphere of product quality and the achievement of 'zero defects' has clearly demonstrated that quality and commitment are inseparable.

Motivation and the Design of Individual Jobs

The individual worker's level of motivation and commitment to the organisation will to a considerable extent reflect his or her satisfaction with the job itself: the actual work he or she is required to do.

Taylorism

In designing jobs managers are usually trying to maximise productivity. The traditional approach is typified by the work of Frederick Taylor (1911), whose approach was based on the twin assumptions that workers were essentially stupid and lazy.

An engineer from Philadelphia who trained as a machinist, Taylor was appalled by the inefficiency of the industrial practices he witnessed and set out to demonstrate how managers and workers could benefit by adopting a more 'scientific' approach. He felt that inefficiency was caused by what he called systematic soldiering, or the deliberate restriction of output by workers anxious to sustain their employment. Soldiering was easy because management control was weak, and because discretion over work methods was left to individual workers, who wasted time and effort with inefficient working rules of thumb. Managers expected their employees to have the appropriate skills for the work they were given, or to learn what to do from those around them. Notions of systematic job specifications, clearly established responsibilities, and training needs analysis were not appreciated. Taylor sought to change that.

He argued that manual and mental work should be separated. Management, he claimed, should specialise in planning and organising work, and workers should specialise in actually doing it. Taylor regarded this as a way of ensuring industrial harmony, as everyone would know clearly what was expected of them and what their responsibilities were. He also saw the clear advantages in making individuals specialise in activities in which they would became expert and highly proficient.

His technique for designing manual jobs involved the following steps. First, decide the optimum degree of task fragmentation, breaking down complex jobs into their simple component parts. Second, determine the most efficient way of performing each part of the work. Studies should be carried out to discover the one best way of doing each of the fragmented tasks, and to design the layout of the workplace and tools to be used so that unnecessary movements could be eliminated. Finally, select and train employees to carry out the fragmented tasks in exactly the one best way, and reward them for above-average performance.

Clearly, task fragmentation can have a number of advantages for the organisation that adopts this approach. Individual workers do not need to be given expensive and time-consuming training, and those who leave or who prove to be unreliable can easily be replaced. Specialisation in one small task makes it possible for people to work very fast at it. Less skilled work is lower paid work. And it is easier to observe and control workers doing simple activities.

At the same time, task fragmentation gives rise to serious motivational problems. The work is repetitive and boring. The contribution of the individual to the work of the organisation as a whole is comparatively meaningless. Monotony can lead to apathy, dissatisfaction and carelessness.

The most frequently quoted research findings on the subject of job design and employee motivation are those of Fred Herzberg (1966). His research team asked people to describe times when they had been particularly happy and unhappy at work. When people talked of times when they had been unhappy the things they mentioned fell mainly under the following headings:

● company policy and administration;

● supervision (technical);

- salary;

- interpersonal relations (supervisory);

- working conditions.

On the other hand, when people described occasions when they were particularly happy the things they talked about were grouped as follows:

- achievement;

- recognition;

- the work itself;

- responsibility.

The two lists are clearly different: they refer to quite different kinds of experience; they are not opposite ends of the same scale. The implication is evident. If management does things to improve working conditions, or raises salaries (what Herzberg calls 'hygiene' factors), grounds for dissatisfaction may be removed but nothing will have been done to create positive motivation. To raise motivation management must pay attention to the nature of the work itself, the extent to which it gives people a sense of achievement and the ways in which people are given recognition for their achievements.

Herzberg's findings have been replicated by some researchers but challenged by others. The most valid challenge is based on evidence that workers from different socio-economic or educational backgrounds or in different cultural settings are motivated in different ways, indicating that human motivation is a complex matter not capable of being reduced to a simple formula.

Designing Organisations

What is important is to try to develop insight into the motivation of particular groups of workers and design the organisation in which they work accordingly.

Job-design experiments in Norway in the 1960s (Emery, 1967) resulted in a set of criteria for designing motivating jobs which is still useful today:

- At the level of the individual:

  1 *Optimum variety*   Avoiding extremes of monotonous repetition leading to boredom and fatigue and over-varied work leading to inefficiency and stress.

  2 *Meaningful work*   A pattern of interdependent activities that result in an overall task which is meaningful – a recognisable component or sub-assembly, for example, or a report which has been typed, corrected, reproduced and bound.

  3 *Optimum length of work cycle*   Too short, and too much time is spent finishing off and starting up – inefficient and frustrating. Too long, and boredom and fatigue set in again.

  4 Some scope for *influencing quantity and quality of outputs*   Although minimum standards may have to be imposed by management, workers are more likely to try to exceed these if given the freedom to set themselves higher standards.

  5 *Knowledge of results*   Whether targets are externally or self-imposed the reinforcement of the achievement drive by providing knowledge of results is an important motivation.

6 *Respect*   The job should be so designed and described that the performance of it engenders respect for the skill, care, service, effort or strength of the performer.

7 *Contribution*   The contribution of the job to company objectives and/or to customer service should be clear.

- At the level of the group:

1 *Interdependence*   Reinforce satisfying group cohesion by means of interacting tasks, job rotation systems, ease of communication between co-workers and physical layout of workstations.

2 *Mutual support*   Where tasks involve danger, stress from other sources, separation from families, etc., provide group support for individuals through such devices as strong group identity, opportunity for off-duty group activities, supportive leadership styles, etc.

3 *Relative autonomy*   The group should be given some degree of responsibility for task allocation, discipline, output norms and quality standards within the boundaries of its own sphere of operations.

Four well-tried approaches to job design which minimise standardisation, specialisation and controls are known as job rotation, job enlargement, job enrichment and autonomous group working.

Job rotation aims at improving motivation by increasing the variety of tasks and reducing monotony. Workers move from one task to another either on the basis of a systematic rota worked out by management or, less formally, on a job-swapping basis by agreement with co-workers.

Job enlargement involves giving each employee a range of tasks as part of his or her normal pattern of working. This is sometimes known as *horizontal* job enlargement.

Job enrichment, also known as *vertical* job enlargement, involves giving each worker additional roles such as inspection, supervision or after-sales service.

Autonomous group working, as the name implies, involves the creation of self-managed multi-skilled teams of workers responsible for more or less complete tasks, such as vehicle assembly. Autonomous working groups were pioneered in the automotive industry by Volvo in Sweden in the 1960s. A more recent example quoted by Tom Peters (1987) is General Motors' Cadillac plant at Livonia, Michigan.

This approach has the following characteristics.

- Every employee is assigned to a small group of eight to fifteen people, known as a 'business team'.

- Each team develops its own indicators of its performance.

- Each team meets weekly to review performance.

- Most awards for suggestions reflect ideas put forward by teams.

- Support for one's team counts in individual performance appraisal.

- Job specialisation has been more or less eliminated and there is a pay-for-knowledge incentive scheme to encourage employees to acquire new skills.

- Second-line supervision (general foreman) has been completely eliminated, while the number of first-line foremen has been reduced by 40 per cent and their job title changed to 'team co-ordinator'.

The most celebrated European examples of experiments in job design have been at Philips (job enlargement), ICI (job enrichment) and Volvo (autonomous work groups). While the leading UK centre for research and ideas was the Tavistock Institute, in the USA the leading advocates of improving motivation through job design have been Fred Herzberg, and Lou Davis of the Center for the Quality of Working Life. The best-publicised US applications were in AT&T, which carried out nineteen job enrichment projects in the 1960s, affecting over 1,000 employees.

Among other US companies reporting beneficial results from incorporating human factor considerations into job design are Texas Instruments, PPG Industries, Monsanto, Syntex, the Oldsmobile Division of General Motors, Corning, Alcan and Kaiser Aluminum.

The benefits included reduced absenteeism, labour turnover and overtime, reductions in staff numbers, increases in production, productivity and earnings, reductions in supervision, increased sales, reduced wastage, quality improvements, less sickness and improved time-keeping.

During the 1970s and early 1980s interest in job design and its relationship to motivation largely died away. This was partly because the clear 'hard' short-term gains from traditional task specialisation – reductions in work in progress and throughput times, reduced space requirements and simplified production control – were believed to outweigh 'softer' considerations of motivation and commitment. In addition, the 'Hawthorne effect' meant that initial gains in output or quality from job enrichment experiments proved not always to be sustainable. Finally, new attitudes and approaches to employee motivation ensured that many of the principles of job design that emerged from the researches and well-publicised experiments have been adopted as normal managerial practice so that forms of job enrichment are being practised today as a matter of course.

More recently, however, interest is reviving, particularly in North America, where some of the most successful attempts to meet Japanese competition have involved radical changes in job design in order to raise levels of motivation and commitment.

Rewards Systems and Motivation

Employee motivation is clearly the central issue when it comes to the design of the organisation's rewards system. As always in the sphere of organisation design, there are many approaches to choose from, and what works well in one situation can fail completely in another.

The Traditional Approach

The traditional approach to reward has been to relate pay and other benefits to characteristics of jobs, such as levels of skill or qualification required, level of responsibility carried, degree of danger involved, working conditions and unsocial hours. Elaborate systems of job evaluation have been developed to enable comparisons and rankings of jobs to be carried out within organisations, while at the same time the evaluation of such characteristics in the wider society is reflected in the 'market rates' attached to various job classifications.

In traditional rewards systems of the kind found in bureaucracies there is a pay rate or scale associated with each job, together with a differential allocation of the tangible or intangible rewards – such as level of pension benefit, private health insurance, company car and various symbols of status. Such rewards are relatively fixed regardless of how well the job is performed, but benefits attached to a particular job frequently increase with length of service. The fairness or legitimacy of such systems is defended on the one hand by demonstrating the elaborate and comprehensive nature and hence the 'objectivity' of the system of job evaluation in use and, on the other, by pointing to the 'market rate' for jobs in the outside world.

Such a system clearly does not address the issue of individual motivation to achieve outstanding performance. Either it is assumed that individuals will be adequately motivated by receiving rewards that are seen to be based on objective criteria or it is believed that motivation is derived primarily from quite different aspects of organisation life and that provided there is no serious dissatisfaction with pay and benefits these things are largely irrelevant from the viewpoint of motivation.

Designing Organisations

Merit Pay and Performance-Related Remuneration

Under this approach people are assigned a basic salary, or wage, and rewards package on the basis of job classification but achieve annual increases above this level as a consequence of assessments of their contribution, performance or 'merit'. The perceived 'fairness' or legitimacy of this approach depends on a number of factors. First, there is the extent to which performance is capable of objective assessment or measurement; jobs obviously vary to a considerable extent in relation to this criterion. Second, the successful completion of some tasks calls for a team effort – in such instances it is very difficult to determine the relative contribution of individual team members. Third, organisation cultures vary a great deal – in some there is the kind of individualistic culture in which individual merit pay is seen as totally appropriate whereas in other cultures the approach is seen as divisive.

Rosabeth Moss Kanter (1989) points out that in a Conference Board survey in the USA around 90 per cent of companies rated individual performance as the chief factor determining pay increases, yet the majority of employees surveyed by the Opinion Research Corporation saw little connection between contribution and subsequent pay increases.

Some schemes are criticised on the grounds that the increases are too small to be significant – 10 to 15 per cent is suggested as the threshold at which there begins to be real reinforcement of high-level performance. Another weakness of such schemes is the reluctance shown by managers and supervisors when it comes to making sharp distinctions between the performance levels achieved by their subordinates. They tend to take the easy way out and rate virtually everybody 'above average'. Also, managers tend to fight for high ratings for their own team members relative to members of other groups in the organisation.

Profit-Sharing Bonuses

The inclusion in the rewards package of a bonus reflecting company performance or profitability is a growing trend. Such one-time payments, because they do not increase basic salary, do not add to fixed costs.

The difficulties with this approach are obvious, however. First, there is no real link between individual effort or performance and reward. If the bonus is paid out to all employees, those who did an outstanding job receive no more than those who did just enough to avoid being fired. Also, in a year in which a consumer boom or the failure of a competitor turns out to be the main cause for increased profits, where is the rationale for rewarding employees for their contribution? If the bonus is to be sufficiently large to affect motivation, is it justifiable to expect low-paid employees to put a significant proportion of their incomes at risk? When paying the mortgage is dependent upon the company achieving its profit targets in a recession year the individual may feel powerless and alienated.

Single Status

In virtually every country of the world non-manual, or white collar, work has traditionally carried with it a higher status and better terms and conditions of work than manual, or blue collar, work. This status divide has been particularly strong and durable in Britain. White collar status is reflected in hours of work, degree of job security, being salaried rather than paid an hourly rate, enjoying better pension rights, sickness benefits and holidays, having incremental pay scales and in many instances separate canteen arrangements.

In the past two decades more and more organisations have come to see the status gap as an obstacle to establishing full trust and co-operation between management and shop-floor employees. In consequence there are now many examples of moves either partly or wholly to single status or harmonisation of terms and conditions of employment for all workers.

Price (1989) gives examples of recent successful single-status deals in the UK. One, at Tioxide UK in 1987, involved the withdrawal of recognition of the Transport and General Workers' Union, a totally new payments system including a profit-related element and complete flexibility with no demarcation between jobs.

At Johnson and Johnson harmonisation was carried out step by step between 1974 and 1982, different aspects of conditions of employment such as pensions, holidays and sick pay arrangements being tackled in turn. Full harmonisation followed, involving pay structures, replacing individual incentives for manual workers with across-the-board group incentives and profit-sharing schemes, and the allocation of new responsibilities to supervisory staff.

Advantage is often taken of the opportunity of starting afresh on a greenfield site, as in the case of BICC Optical Cables at Whiston, where a seven-grade integrated pay structure covering all employees was introduced alongside common pay and performance review systems and harmonised conditions of employment.

Without doubt many British firms as well as enterprises in other Western countries have been influenced by the success achieved by Japanese companies operating locally. The practices at companies such as Nissan, Toshiba and Hitachi of no separate canteens or car parks, no distinctions of dress and a general absence of status 'perks' have been strongly linked to their achievement of harmonious labour relations and remarkably high standards of productivity and quality.

Quality Circles

Confidence in traditional approaches to job design, and in particular the specialised and standardised nature of work on the assembly line, has been dented in the past decade by the extent to which the Japanese automobile industry has penetrated the US market. Although the Japanese have benefited from a shift in consumer preference towards smaller cars with lower fuel consumption, few people doubt that a major factor has been superior quality and productivity by the Japanese, and it is generally accepted that worker motivation rather than superior technology or production planning is the most significant influence on this. In consequence attention has focused on the means by which the Japanese manufacturers sustain a high level of motivation. While it is recognised that cultural factors play a large part, it is also accepted that organisational techniques, and in particular quality circles, are of considerable importance.

Quality circles first developed in Japan but today there are thousands in other parts of the world. A quality circle normally consists of a group of between four and twelve people, drawn from the same part of the organisation, who *voluntarily* meet on a regular basis to identify, investigate and solve their own work-related problems – particularly those to do with the achievement of quality standards. The solutions they develop are presented to management and, if accepted, the group will usually be involved in their implementation.

In practice there are considerable variations between organisations in the precise arrangements adopted – in some instances even the name 'quality circles' is not used. Three essential elements are, however, usually present: a steering group of some kind which oversees the whole process, a facilitator, and properly trained circle leaders.

The steering group is sometimes chaired by the most senior line manager on site but in other cases by a workers' representative, the personnel manager or a trade union officer. Its membership will normally include line managers, shop-floor workers, quality specialists and trade union officers where appropriate.

The facilitator – and in the larger companies this is often a full-time job – links the steering committee to the actual circles on an ongoing basis. He or she needs strongly developed communications, counselling and training skills. The facilitator acts as coach to the circle leaders and groups, attends meetings, provides training, gives support and ensures the momentum of the programme is maintained.

[104]

The circle group leader is sometimes but not always the line supervisor of the members of the group. The main thing is that he or she is adequately trained for the role.

Experience has shown that for quality circles to be fully effective the following additional factors need to be present:

- commitment and support from top management must be visible and continuing;

- operational managers must be responsive and co-operative;

- the preparation and training must be thorough;

- there must be adequate recognition of successes achieved;

- the company culture must be capable of supporting a participative approach;

- the pre-existing climate of employee relations must be reasonably favourable;

- all parties must be prepared to be patient and persistent and not expect miracles overnight.

Black and Decker introduced its first quality circle in the UK in 1980 and had around fifty operating by 1985. At its Spennymoor, County Durham plant, opened in 1965, there was an established tradition of efficiency, high productivity and excellent labour relations. Quality circles built on this firm foundation and tapped the ideas and energy of the workforce in new ways. In one instance a woman employee discussed with her husband (an industrial chemist) a problem to do with the oxidisation of commutators in stockrooms. Their experiments at home led to her circle's recommending an economic solution to the problem. Another circle recommended recycling worn cutting tools instead of replacing them, leading to considerable cost savings.

Quality circles played a part in the dramatic improvements in quality of service and business performance at British Airways. Here the groups are called 'customer first' teams. The group leaders are invited to sit in on regular management workshops in order to ensure a good two-way flow of communication. Examples of the achievements of British Airways' teams include improved arrangements for tracing and delivering lost baggage, improved presentation of flight information to passengers, and better ways of dealing with unaccompanied children.

At Eaton Limited, the UK subsidiary of the Eaton Corporation, the term 'problem-solving groups' is used. They were set up in 1980. One project led to annual savings running well into six figures. The starting point was the frustration of one group member whose work area was cluttered with parts awaiting recovery. These were rejects resulting from occasional difficulty in fitting a threaded plug into the end of a shaft. The eventual solution, which involved a change in materials, resulted in less waste and a better production process. The new methods were adopted elsewhere in the group.

Although it is natural to look for examples of cost savings or measurable improvements in quality consequent upon the introduction of quality circles many companies with some years' experience in using them stress that the more important gain is the overall change in organisational climate: a new spirit of co-operation between management and workforce. For example, running quality circles at Josiah Wedgwood & Son Ltd costs over £100,000 a year. Although clearly identifiable cost savings amount to a greater sum the company's quality circle facilitator believes the real benefit lies in the change in people's enthusiasm and attitude towards their work.

When quality circles fail to produce results, according to Tom Peters (1987) it is for one or more of the following reasons:

- inadequate training and preparation for all concerned;
- lack of sufficiently powerful incentives;
- lack of communication and top management support;
- failure to implement sensible recommendations;
- failure to monitor and feed back results;
- trying to move too fast – 'instant miracles'.

Training and Motivation

Peters (1987) emphasises the seriousness with which Japanese companies approach shop-floor training and the fact that it is concerned as much with 'empowering' employees in the motivational sense as with the transfer of skills and technology. He argues that most US and European organisations regard motivation and job satisfaction as something to keep people contented, whereas the Japanese see them empowering employees to transform performance. He quotes the example of the Nissan plant start-up in Smyrna, Tennessee where $63 million was spent on training 2,000 workers – over $30,000 a head before a single car came off the line. It is hard to imagine many US or European organisations making such a huge investment in human capital.

The use of training primarily as a means for changing attitudes and building a committed workforce is, in any event, a relatively recent development. In Britain even very large organisations such as British Airways and the clearing banks have provided training for all employees in the field of customer service. This training is not intended so much to impart specific job-related skills but rather to instil in the participants an emotional commitment to service, to quality and to organisational success.

Security of Employment

It is characteristic of a number of high-performance organisations, particularly in the USA and Japan but more rarely in Europe, that they offer a virtual guarantee of security of employment. In effect what they are doing is saying that all employees – not just management and the top executive team – have full membership in the organisation and, once admitted to membership, acquire certain rights, the right to security of employment being one of the most important.

The US companies which have such a policy include IBM, S. C. Johnson (of Johnson's Wax fame), Hewlett-Packard, Hallmark, Digital and Federal Express. Among the advantages such companies perceive as resulting from policies of this kind are:

- willingness to accept change, to volunteer ideas which raise productivity, and to give up restrictive practices;

- co-operation and flexibility generally, including willingness to be retrained;

- costs of redundancy and recruiting and training 'green' labour are virtually eliminated.

Employee Share Ownership

Security of employment is frequently accompanied by other features of organisational design which reinforce its motivational aspects. One particularly important one is an employee share ownership plan (ESOP).

In the USA around eighty of the Fortune 500 top companies have introduced ESOPs, including Procter & Gamble, ITT, Xerox and Delta. PepsiCo became the first Fortune 500 company to introduce employee stock options. Each year workers receive options equal to 10 per cent of their wages or salaries priced at the stock's current value. Employees can exercise their options at any time within ten years after the options are granted. When they do the company will pay out the profit in the form of PepsiCo shares. If employees hold their stock rather than sell it employee ownership will grow at a rate of about 4 per cent a decade.

In 1979 just thirty employees share schemes had been approved by the UK Inland Revenue. There are now more than 4,000, covering 1.5 million workers.

[109]

Motivation and Culture

Every organisation has its characteristic culture – analogous to the human personality – although some cultures are much stronger and hence more readily described than others. The culture reflects a whole range of intangible factors, including style of management, preferred goals and preferred means of achieving them, types of people who belong to the organisation, particular traditions or myths from the organisation's past and the legacies of particularly strong personalities. A business which is, or has been in the recent past, a family concern, will certainly have a quite different culture from one with wide share ownership and entirely professional management. Such an organisation will in turn have a radically different culture from that of a government department or a charity. This much is obvious. Yet two organisations with very similar tasks, both in public ownership and both of similar size, can also have radically different cultures.

Some of the words used to describe corporate cultures are listed below.

Anti-intellectual	Authoritarian
Bureaucratic	Caring
Competitive	Conformist
Creative	Egalitarian
Élitist	Entrepreneurial
Fire-fighting	Friendly
Hierarchical	Hire and fire
Innovative	Macho
Meritocratic	Militaristic
Participative	Paternalistic

Political	Production-oriented
Punitive	Risk-avoiding
Technocratic	Traditional
Trusting	Work hard/play hard

The view is rapidly gaining ground that corporate culture has an even more powerful influence on employee motivation than have structural factors such as the design of jobs or work groups or systems such as incentive schemes. This view reflects the spectacular successes achieved by certain companies with strong and distinctive cultures, where there is convincing evidence that the success largely reflects an unusually high level of employee commitment and motivation.

Tom Peters has publicised a number of American examples in a whole series of books and videos featuring a wide range of organisations in terms of size, industry, public and private sector and ownership. Peters's US role models include Apple Computer, Cray Research, Federal Express, The Limited, Milliken, Stew Leonard's Supermarket, Johnsonville Sausage and Worthington Industries.

In Britain the creation of a service culture was central to the improvement in British Airways' performance, and many organisations are now trying (not always successfully) to emulate this achievement by means of cultural change.

What kind of culture is it that can have a radical effect on the attitudes and commitment of employees? The answer appears to lie primarily in the sphere of values. Differences in corporate cultures reflect differences in values. Employees are 'turned on' and become committed when:

[111]

- the values are clearly articulated and constantly reinforced;
- the values are ones they can identify with and adopt as their own;
- top management 'lives' the values.

The example of the Procter & Gamble plant, at the beginning of this chapter, showed how effective values can be. In that case every employee carried a statement of values on a plastic card. The rapidly growing French electronics firm Metrologie lists its values as:

- communication;
- equality;
- experience and risk (learning by mistakes);
- creativity;
- responsibility;
- autonomy;
- respect for customers.

It attributes its spectacular growth and above average profitability to the creation of a distinctive culture based on these values.

Other companies express their core values much more succinctly – British Airways uses the expression 'putting people first'. Thomas J. Watson, founder of IBM, argued that

the basic philosophy, spirit and drive of an organization have far more to do with its relative achievements than do technological or economic resources, organizational structures, innovation and timing. All these things weigh heavily on success but they are, I think, transcended by how strongly the people in the organization believe in its basic precepts and how faithfully they carry them out.

$$\boxed{6}$$

Organising for Innovation and Flexibility

3M – an Innovative Organisation

3M is probably the most frequently cited example of an innovative organisation. Originating from a base of sandpaper and tape its products today can be counted in thousands, ranging from Post-it Notes to heart–lung machines. It is a giant corporation, with sales in excess of $10 billion, yet it is more innovative and flexible than most small businesses. 3M is an excellent example of an approach to organisation design in which structure, systems and culture interact in a mutually reinforcing way to produce the desired outcomes.

In structure the emphasis is on a large number (over forty) of relatively small, autonomous product divisions. Median plant size is 115 employees; of ninety plants only five employ over 1,000 people. Organisational roles include 'executive champions' committed to supporting new ventures. The career structure provides separate promotion opportunities for innovators.

Among the systems and procedures in use are the following:

- *The 25 per cent rule*   25 per cent of sales must come

from products developed within the previous five years. (In 1988, 32 per cent of sales qualified.)

- *The 15 per cent rule*   Allows personnel to spend up to 15 per cent of the working week at their own discretion, provided the activity is product-related.

- *Genesis grants*   These give researchers up to $50,000 to develop projects past the idea stage. A panel of technical experts and scientists awards as many as ninety each year.

- *Golden Step Awards*   For products that achieve sales of $2 million, at a profit, within three years of launch. In 1981, when Post-it Notes won an award, thirteen other products did too. In 1987 over fifty new products qualified.

The innovative culture is long standing and is founded on legends and heroes of the past. The freedom to fail, for example, is based on the story of Francis T. Okie's idea, in 1922, of selling sandpaper as a substitute for razors. Okie, who persisted in sanding his own face (or so the legend goes) was able to champion such a crazy idea and yet keep his job. In the end he triumphed by inventing a waterproof sandpaper which became a winner for the company. Features of the 3M culture include:

- employees are trusted; control is through peer review and feedback;

- getting close to the customer;

- be patient and give new ideas and products enough time;

- have respect for other people's ideas;
- openness in communication;
- 'growing own timber' – rarely recruiting from outside and never at senior level.

Other innovative companies in North America include Rubbomaid (30 per cent of sales must come from products developed in the previous five years), Hewlett-Packard (researchers are able to spend 10 per cent of their time on their own pet projects; there is twenty-four-hour access to laboratories and equipment; operates in small divisions), Dow Corning (forms research partnerships with customers), Merck (gives researchers time and resources to pursue high-risk/high pay-off projects), General Electric (develops products jointly with customers), Johnson and Johnson (freedom to fail; autonomous operating units) and Black and Decker (advisory councils get new product ideas from customers).

Innovation and Structure

Tom Peters and Nancy Austin (1985) argue that we must learn to design organisations that take into account the 'irreducible sloppiness' of the innovation process. They point out that most innovation occurs in unplanned unpredictable ways, often in industries quite unrelated to the nature of the innovation. They quote the study by John Jewkes and others (1969), who analysed fifty-eight major inventions ranging from ballpoint pens to penicillin. At least forty-six occurred in the 'wrong place', i.e.

[116]

in very small firms, by individuals, by people in 'out-groups' in large companies or in large companies in the wrong industry. Examples include Kodachrome, invented by two musicians; continuous casting of steel by a watchmaker experimenting with brass casting; synthetic detergents by dye-stuff chemists.

There is overwhelming evidence that much if not most practical innovation in large companies is the result of small groups of six to twenty-five people supported by a product champion but frequently acting in secret or in defiance of company policy – what Peters calls a 'skunkwork'. Examples include Ericsson's AXE digital switching system, the UNIX operating system of AT&T, even the first locomotive built by General Electric and the basic oxygen furnace by Nippon Kokan (at the time Japan's third largest steel company).

Decentralisation is clearly an important component in success. Johnson and Johnson's phrase is 'growing big by staying small'. IBM, PepsiCo, Hewlett-Packard, Raychem, Mars and Citicorp all follow the same organisational strategy. In Peters's words, for them 'the structure *is* the strategy'. The trend is toward lean corporate staffs and increasingly small operating divisions.

Another common feature of the organisation structure in highly innovative firms is the close interaction and early involvement of marketing and manufacturing personnel with research and development staff. Hewlett-Packard has adopted the principle of the 'triad' development team: design engineers, marketing and manufacturing people being full-time partners in product development from early in the design phase.

Analysis also shows that a great many – perhaps the majority – of ideas for new products originate with users.

[117]

This highlights the need for strong organisational links between innovative companies and potential lead users of new products.

Venture Organisations

This approach involves setting up a semi-independent venture organisation within the company. If designated a profit centre, it can carry out commissioned research and development for operating divisions, which concentrate on manufacturing and marketing existing products. The unit may also develop new products, not suitable for or not acceptable to the parent company, which may be licensed or sold to other companies.

Venture organisations have the advantage that they radically separate ongoing business from research and development. This creates favourable conditions for company creativity but causes problems when it comes to translating a new concept into a manufactured product tailored to the needs of the markets. It helps to exchange personnel between the venture organisation and the operating divisions.

The 'Innovation Champion'

Simon Majaro (1988) cites the case of a major UK-based international company in the fast-moving consumer goods field which appointed a director of innovation with main board status. His task was to play a pivotal role in facilitating a free flow of innovative ideas between subsidiaries in different countries, collecting and disseminating ideas and setting up mechanisms for motivating people to develop new ideas and come forward with them.

Systems and Procedures for Stimulating Innovation

Suggestion Schemes

Majaro (1988) gives the example of a British engineering firm which developed a system known as the 'Treasure Chest'. The first stage of the process was to issue a little red book (based on the model of the *Thoughts of Chairman Mao*) which emphasised the importance of creativity and the role that every member of the organisation could play in stimulating it. Suggestion boxes ('treasure chests') were then installed in prominent positions in the company's premises. Huge charts showing the number of ideas submitted monthly were installed in the main plants and offices. A screening committee chaired by the chief executive was set up to evaluate the ideas; its membership included shop-floor representatives. Rewards and recognition were provided for those who submitted winning ideas.

This represents an unusually imaginative approach to the basic concept of the suggestion scheme. The underlying assumption is that a mass of creative ideas are locked up in people's minds and that all that is needed is a mechanism for encouraging people to come forward with them. Most companies that use this approach find, however, that after the first flurry of enthusiasm the

[119]

number of ideas submitted rapidly dies away. Majaro suggests several reasons why suggestion schemes fail.

- *Poor promotion of the scheme* The basic rules of sound marketing apply with equal force to an internal activity of this kind as they do to persuading external customers to buy the product.

- *Lack of motivation* The first requirement is that employees identify with the goals of the organisation. Beyond this there should be specific rewards for winning ideas, but these rewards need not be financial. Certificates of achievement, personal letters from the chief executive or publicity in the company newspaper can be even more effective than cash payments.

- *Lack of feedback* If individuals who submit what they naturally believe to be good ideas never receive a reaction their enthusiasm will be quickly extinguished; so too if a significant time elapses without any tangible results.

- *Poor screening of ideas* This is a very difficult area since the whole process is so subjective. Who, in the last analysis, is best qualified to carry out the evaluation process? Without doubt many brilliant ideas fail to get past screening committees made up of people with inadequate imagination, courage or vision. It is difficult for members of screening panels to overcome a natural tendency to adopt a negative attitude to the ideas of others, and the well-known 'not invented here' syndrome has a very powerful effect.

Well-thought-out schemes will anticipate these problems and involve means of overcoming them.

Brainstorming

Many organisations make use of the procedure known as brainstorming, first developed by Alex Osborn (1953) and described in his book *Applied Imagination*. Osborn first used the technique in his company in 1939. A brainstorming session is an *informal* group activity specifically designed to generate useful creative ideas. There are four basic rules:

- Judgements are barred. Ideas are not criticised or ruled out until a later stage.

- 'Free-wheeling' is encouraged. The wilder the idea the better since it is easier to 'tame down' than to 'think up'.

- Quantity is wanted – the bigger the list the greater the likelihood it will contain winners.

- Combination and improvement are to be encouraged – as well as putting their own ideas forward participants should suggest how the ideas of others can be turned into better ideas.

Osborn's technique has stood the test of time. It is best used when the following conditions apply.

- The problem is *specific* rather than general, *simple* rather than complex, *familiar* rather than novel.

- The will to solve the problem is present among those responsible for its resolution.

- Relationships between group members are such that participants will not be inhibited or afraid of making fools of themselves.

Creating an Innovative Culture

The approach to innovation which is based on structures and systems alone is unlikely to be wholly successful. The creation of a culture or organisational climate conducive to innovation is a vital component of strategy. There are, of course, no hard and fast guidelines for the development of such a culture, but some ideas based on the experience of highly innovative organisations can be set out.

First, there are several ways in which the top management of an organisation can convey how strongly they value creativity and innovation. These include sponsoring artists, bringing their work into the organisation and sponsoring competitions in local schools to encourage inventiveness. Second, individuality and self-expression can be encouraged by such simple means as not imposing a uniform way of dressing, not insisting on standard office furnishing and offering key personnel a wide choice of company car.

Third, the free flow of ideas can be greatly enhanced by de-emphasising hierarchy, status and seniority, and by providing frequent opportunities for people from different parts of the organisation to meet informally yet not purely for social purposes.

Fourth, the value placed on creativity and innovation can be symbolised by the presentation of corporate image and 'house style' in such things as the organisation's literature and stationery, the colour schemes used in its buildings, the 'livery' of its vehicle fleet, the style used in its TV advertising, and so on.

Finally, it is helpful to expose members of the organisation to sources of ideas or perspectives on the world from a variety of backgrounds. To this end networks can be built, made up of philosophers, social scientists, inventors, radical thinkers, writers and others whose ideas can powerfully stimulate the thinking of those who would otherwise become locked into the particular mind set of a single organisational environment.

Flexible Organisations – Building in the Capacity to Respond to a Changing Environment

Forces which are creating the need for flexibility in today's organisations include:

- global markets and growing international competitiveness;

- changes in the political–legal sphere: deregulation, environmental conservation;

- impact of mergers and acquisitions – leading to increases in size and complexity;

- social changes – values, social structure, demographic and lifestyle changes;

- increased availability of information and information processing capability;

- rapid development of new production technologies.

Change under any one of these headings could trigger a need for modification to an organisation's structure or systems. Given the fact that for many firms change is occurring simultaneously and rapidly under all six headings, it is not surprising that stability of structure and systems is the exception rather than the rule and that organisation design has to be seen as an ongoing adaptive process rather than as a task analogous to building a cathedral.

The traditional bureaucratic structure provides a matching internal function for every environmental issue or problem. Marketing, purchasing, distribution, labour relations, public relations and similar functions or departments exist to regulate relationships across the organisation's boundaries. In a turbulent environment, however, problems increasingly arise which cannot be neatly matched with the competence possessed by any one part of the organisation. The lack of congruence between the tidy and clearly differentiated functional cells of the structure and the messy, complex, undifferentiated problems on the outside – to do with such issues as air pollution, consumer health and safety, investigations by government commissions, unwelcome or hostile take-over bids – means that problems go to the wrong departments for resolution or fall into the gaps between departments or that the company moves into a mode of ongoing reorganisation in an endeavour to adapt to a shifting pattern of external pressures and constraints.

Many of the issues or problems, however, are 'one-offs' or temporary in nature. They call for temporary task groups to resolve them. Such groupings for specific *ad hoc* purposes will increasingly form a major part of the structure of organisations.

Hierarchical control systems depend on two factors: accurate feedback of information from operations and relative homogeneity of the types of decisions required. When the same kinds of situation constantly recur managers accumulate useful experience from past errors and successes. When these two conditions are absent hierarchical control is less effective. In today's conditions, involving very varied types of decision and uncertainty in terms of accurate feedback, decisions have to be taken much closer to the front line.

Learning Organisations

In recent years the term 'the learning organisation' has come into use to describe the kind of organisation that is capable of continuous adaptation to changing circumstances.

Organisations are capable of learning in the sense that they can develop competences and maintain them over considerable periods of time despite changes in key personnel and in business conditions during the period. Procter & Gamble has developed this kind of competence in marketing, Marks and Spencer in retailing, and the Mandarin Group in running luxury hotels.

The definition offered by Michael Beck (1989) is that a learning organisation is 'one which facilitates learning and personal development for all its staff whilst continually transforming itself'. This definition emphasises the link between individual learning and organisational learning.

Bo Hedberg (1981) argues convincingly that although organisational learning occurs through individuals it would be wrong to assert that it is merely the sum of the learning by individual members. Although organisations do not have brains in the sense that human beings do, they do have cognitive systems and memories. Just as individuals develop patterns of behaviour and beliefs over time so organisations develop ideologies and ways of doing things. Members come and go and the leadership can change, but certain ideas, practices and beliefs remain stored in the organisation's memory. Standard operating procedures are the organisational equivalent of individuals' behaviour patterns. Customs, symbols and traditions carry the organisation's values. The culture of the firm acts as a learning resource as the organisation's heritage of learning is transmitted to new members through a range of formal and informal induction processes.

Organisations cannot learn except by the process of individual members acquiring knowledge and skills. The learning that individuals achieve, however, becomes transformed into organisational learning when it becomes embedded in some way in the life of the organisation so that it remains as an asset after the individual has moved elsewhere.

Michael Beck's definition also emphasises the developmental and adaptive or transformational role of learning. In a learning organisation the process of learning involves challenging the conventional wisdom rather than receiving it uncritically. New employees may learn 'how things are done around here' but, equally (because the activity is learning, not teaching or being taught), established staff learn from newcomers and top management learn from people at shop-floor level.

Another way of looking at the process that goes on inside the learning organisation is that it is a cycle. The company develops its individuals, broadens their vision, gives them new knowledge, enhances their skills and then in turn learns from the same people how the company can be improved.

If the resultant learning is to be transferred from individuals to the organisation as a whole, mechanisms which enable this to happen must exist. The most common mechanism is to design or modify a system or procedure – a process which obviously involves the risk of building rigidity rather than flexibility into the organisation. The definition reflects this danger by emphasising that the process of transformation should be a *continuing* one. Organisational learning, therefore, is not of the kind which involves a search for absolute truths or the right answers. It is more like learning to be a better chess player in the sense that the learner is driven by a constant desire to improve, learns from mistakes, profits from feedback and knows (with the possible temporary exception of the winner of the world championship) that the time will never come when there is nothing more to be learned.

It is, therefore, important to create a culture or climate in which learning is highly valued, one which is 'open' in the sense that challenging the conventional wisdom is acceptable and one in which risk-taking is encouraged and mistakes are seen as occasions for learning.

[127]

Designing Organisations

The importance of role-modelling by top management in this context cannot be too strongly emphasised. If a learning culture is to be successfully fostered members of the top managment team, including the chief executive, must themselves be seen to be actively involved in learning. They must be prepared to find time to take part in both internal and external programmes as participants, to accept tutorial or mentor roles in company programmes, and above all to be seen to be receptive to new ideas, curious about the environment and questioning of the firm's longest-established and most cherished practices.

Other ways in which the culture can be influenced include:

- incorporating references to the role of learning in company mission statements;

- creating open, upward channels of communication. IBM's Speak Up programme makes it possible for any member of the organisation to ask publicly any question of any member of management – and to be answered publicly.

Facilitating Learning

The conventional view is that learning takes place on training courses. Hopefully it does, but fostering the climate of a learning organisation will involve other strategies for facilitating learning on the job and in less formal ways. Among the most commonly adopted approaches are the following.

[128]

Networking

Making opportunities for people to interact with a much wider network – horizontally, vertically and diagonally – than is possible in the context of normal day-to-day working. At one extreme this can involve taking whole groups of staff off-site for a 'retreat' or 'away day' lasting perhaps one or two days or, less ambitiously, hourly meetings scheduled on a monthly basis.

Feedback

If individuals are to learn from experience they will need feedback in an acceptable form to tell them how well they are doing. This is an issue to be handled in a sensitive manner, since feedback leads to learning only when it is acceptable to the recipient. IBM's approach to counselling and appraisal is a good model of the right approach.

Special assignments

Move people temporarily away from their normal work situation. For example, they may join project teams working on special tasks or, more adventurously, be seconded outside the organisation to gain fresh experience and perspective by working in radically different environments, e.g. in non-profit organisations or in businesses in other countries.

Facilities for Self-Development

Resources and time off for study purposes, financial assistance with costs of education and training not directly linked to the current job, extra pay for extra qualifications, the availability of open learning systems on company premises, the use of mentors or coaches and other support systems: all these can assist individuals to learn and to develop.

'Unlearning' in Organisations

'Unlearning' is more difficult to achieve than learning. It involves the ability to recognise that systems, procedures and behaviours which were in the past associated with successful organisational performance have become inappropriate and even counterproductive and the ability to abandon these in favour of new ones, as yet untried.

The recent history of IBM illustrates how rapidly a change in business conditions can render much of the accumulated experience of an organisation useless. With the rapid development of the market for personal computers IBM had to face the following changes:

Previously	*Now*
● Relatively few customers	Literally millions of customers
● Relatively few competitors	Hundreds – perhaps thousands – of competitors
● Predictable techno-logical change	Explosive rate of techno-logical change
● Foremost impor-tance of hardware	Foremost importance of systems, software and solutions

- Reliance on own   Marketing through busi-
  direct salesforce   ness partners

- Standard terms of   Many ways of doing
  business   business

In adjusting to these new conditions IBM at first encountered considerable difficulties – in the words of chief executive Akers, 'We went off track.' These difficulties reflected the enormous problems associated with 'unlearning' and abandoning practices which over many years had led to IBM's winning a reputation as the world's best-managed corporation.

Summary and Conclusion

Organising for innovation and flexibility gives rise to special problems since there are inherent contradictions between the underlying concepts of organisation – such as order, predictability, routine and standardisation – and the conditions in which creativity will flourish and flexibility prevail. Creativity tends to shun the imposition of order, to seek to evade control. Moreover, when things are most regulated they are most resistant to change. Where innovation and/or the ability to adapt rapidly to changing circumstances are vital for organisational survival and success there is no alternative, however, but to 'unlearn' most of the rules about organisation design developed during an earlier, more stable period and to throw out the time-honoured procedural manuals and systems. This is never an easy thing to do and it is most difficult for very large organisations.

[131]

Designing Organisations

It is noticeable that size is no longer regarded as such a desirable corporate asset as in the past and a growing tendency for companies to decentralise can be identified, even to the extent of divesting large sections of the business.

7

Managing Organisational Change

Introduction

Alvin Toffler (1985) tells how in 1968 he received a telephone call from the corporate headquarters of AT&T. A
vice-president of the company invited him to spend
several years studying the entire huge organisation,
offering free access to every executive on a non-attribut-
able basis, and to address two questions: given the
revolution in telecommunications that was now beginning what should AT&T's mission be and how should it
reorganise itself to carry it out?

Toffler spend four years on the assignment and in 1972
submitted ten bound copies of his report, 'Social Dyna-
mics of the Bell System'. It called for very radical organisational change. Toffler waited in vain for an invitation to
meet the board and discuss his report. The invitation
never came. Although there was no official top management reaction to the document it did not simply gather
dust on the shelves nor was it consigned to the incinera-
tor. Xerox copies began to circulate unofficially through
the management structure and it began to influence
people's thinking.

Three years later Toffler met the new chairman of

Designing Organisations

AT&T at a business dinner and was told that the 'underground' report had broken through to the surface and had been officially distributed widely in the organisation as a means of stimulating a debate about its future strategy.

AT&T provides an excellent example of a need for organisational transformation arising from changes in market conditions. Until 1954 AT&T telephones were standard black. That year they introduced eight colour choices in a standard telephone, and such new products as the Speakerphone, the wall telephone, and the Princess telephone. In the business sector this growing diversity of domestic appliances was matched with a range of increasingly complex internal communications systems. In the late 1950s the company moved into data transmission services. By the early 1970s AT&T was producing approximately 250,000 different service offerings ranging from small optional add-ons to a customised corporate communications system such as that installed at Lockheed at an annual rental of $12 million. By this time the company was producing 1,500 different types of telephone.

To create and assemble these increasingly diverse components and products involved a shift from very long to relatively short production runs. The sub-assemblies being built into communications systems increasingly needed to be individually designed and 'crafted' rather than mass produced. The concept of shorter runs, less routine, more exceptions applied in non-manufacturing areas also. All this increased variety and flexibility created a 'choking sense of complexity'.

These changes in the level of uncertainty generated by new market conditions inevitably meant that AT&T

managers and other employees could no longer rely on pre-existing routines or standard procedures as frequently or as safely as in the past. Increasingly, individuals were faced with situations in which they had to invent a new response.

Just as the factory was invented to pump out standardised products so the bureaucracy was invented to pump out standardised decisions. Bureaucratic systems of organisation can perform a limited range of repetitive functions in a relatively predictable environment. Given greater diversity, variety and uncertainty in task and environment, bureaucracy must be replaced by less formal, more flexible structures – by what Toffler calls 'adhocracy'.

Toffler proposed for AT&T a highly flexible structure made up of a 'framework' and 'modules', conceived as at the centre of a shifting 'constellation' of related companies, agencies and other external bodies. The framework was described as 'thin co-ordinating wiring'. He believed this loose structural form would overcome three common problems in large organisations: organisational mismatch, over-reliance on top-down decision-making and overmanning – 'just plain flab'.

Two Types of Organisational Change

The AT&T case serves to emphasise an important distinction between two types of organisational change.

The first can be described as 'reorganising'. It becomes necessary from time to time in all organisations if they are to adapt to changing circumstances. It can be occasioned by simple growth, by diversification involving new products and new markets, by the introduction of new technology, by the need to respond to new sources of competition or to grasp new business opportunities afforded by deregulation. It may simply be the result of a feeling that it is time to shuffle the pack. Reorganising involves a wide range of decisions and actions: redefining people's roles, creating new ones, regrouping activities, changing reporting relationships, introducing new systems and procedures and modifying or abandoning existing ones. Following such changes certain benefits ideally accrue, such as higher productivity, improved customer service, growth in market share, successful penetration of new markets, and so on.

The objective of reorganising is, however, limited. The aim is to adapt or modify an existing social institution to make it more effective in achieving its goals, but not to alter its fundamental characteristics. For example, if the organisation possesses certain characteristics which taken together could justify describing it as a bureaucracy, the purpose of reorganising is to make it a more efficient bureaucracy, not to transform it into something quite different.

The second type of organisational change has been described as 'organisational transformation'. Here the purpose is clearly to transform the organisation into a radically different form of social institution from that which currently exists. Although many of the same actions and decisions affecting structure and systems will be called for as in the case of reorganisation – changes in roles, groupings, relationships – they will tend to be more radical and far-reaching in nature and involve such processes as reducing the number of levels in the hierarchy or establishing autonomous work groups. Additionally, organisational transformation will always involve bringing about changes in values, attitudes and beliefs – the elements of corporate culture.

Failure to bring about cultural change will doom attempts to effect *radical* change in organisations.

Changing Organisational Culture

This process involves persuading people to abandon their existing beliefs and values, and the behaviours that stem from them, and to adopt new ones.

The first difficulty that arises in practice is to identify the principal characteristics of the existing culture. In most organisations that have been in existence for more than one or two decades a culture will have developed in an unplanned, unconscious way, as a consequence of the interaction of a whole series of factors. In the UK, for example, the culture of organisations will be influenced by, among other things, the following.

- The geographical roots of the corporation – the City of London, the industrial north of England, the Scottish lowlands, etc.

- The sources of recruitment of élites: does the organisation have a tradition of graduate entry or, as in the case of the police, is there a tradition of promotion from the ranks? Do the top people tend to be recruited from a particular social class, as is the case with certain regiments in the British army?

[137]

Designing Organisations

- The nature of the organisation's basic activity: is the work dangerous or dirty? Does it call for brain or brawn? Can women do it as well as or better than men?

- What have been the business conditions during the organisation's formative years? Fierce competition or cosy monopoly? Exposure to market forces or cocooning within the public sector? Operating in steady markets or in ones subject to sharp fluctuations in demand and fashion?

- What has been the organisation's record of achievement? Can it look back on a great and glorious past?

Many large organisations that came into being in the early years of the twentieth century in Britain grew up in conditions which have left permanent traces in their cultures. These conditions included:

- a particularly rigid structure of social classes in the community characterised by a considerable status gap between those who, however skilled, worked principally with their hands and those who, even at the low skill level of the clerical worker, worked with their brains;

- a highly protected home market supplemented by Commonwealth preference that made it possible to evade intense competition through a combination of cartels at home and/or absence of serious competition overseas;

- a strong tradition of mistrust of professionals and respect for the gifted amateur;

- ascribing low status to a career in industry or in the engineering professions relative to careers in other professions (law, medicine), higher education, the civil service, the City or the Church;

- a social context in which women were expected to concentrate their lives and energies on the home: their occupational roles were almost exclusively confined to being secretaries, nurses, shop assistants or assembly workers in light industry;

- a world in which consumers were expected to be (and usually were) relatively easily satisfied and in which to complain about quality or service was regarded as a sign of a bad upbringing. A world in which a chronic inability to satisfy potential demand was intensified by acute shortages in two world wars, breeding a 'take it or leave it' attitude.

The cultural features of many organisations which developed during this period are described below.

- Complacency bordering on arrogance: 'We belong to a great and powerful organisation with an unbroken record of prosperity and with products that are household names. What could we possibly learn from sources outside our own concern?'

- Conservatism: 'The methods that have brought us success in the past will stand us in good stead for the future.'

Designing Organisations

- Production orientation: 'Marketing is just another word for selling and sales representatives – commercial travellers – are low forms of life.'

- Concern for status and seniority: the company car, a private reserved parking space, membership of the senior lunch mess, one's own secretary – these are the greatest prizes to be won.

- A secretive, closed climate in which information is seen as a source of power and control, under no circumstances to be widely shared: in such organisations even the most trivial communications pass in sealed envelopes marked 'confidential'.

- A surprising degree of tolerance of incompetence, particularly on the part of 'loyal' long-serving members of the organisation: there is little effort to manage performance or to deal with problems such as alcoholism.

- A marked lack of sophistication in human resource management: shop-floor workers are thought of as 'hands'. If motivation is considered at all it is assumed that only financial incentives are likely to be effective. Personnel policies support the blue collar/white collar status divide. Fluctuations in business conditions are dealt with by laying off hourly-paid workers during periods of slack demand.

- The steady growth of routine practices and procedures to cover every eventuality has led to a tendency to treat the rules as ends in themselves rather than as means to an end. The phrase 'it's more than my job's worth . . .' is frequently heard.

[140]

- Women rarely prosper in such organisations: 'Their place is in the home.'

It was the development of bureaucratic cultures with features closely resembling these that led to the stagnation of much of British industry and its loss of international competitiveness during the 1960s and 1970s. The characteristics described above were particularly salient in motor vehicle manufacturing, in the larger textile and clothing manufacturers, in companies the very names of which betrayed their origins and outlooks: *Imperial* Tobacco, *Imperial* Chemical Industries and *Burmah* Oil.

Today, in the new climate of global competition, set in a more egalitarian society and one in which women increasingly enjoy equality of opportunity, in a world in which the customer is king and in the context of a growing recognition of the vital role of industry in the life of the nation, new, more appropriate cultures are being shaped. The old values are being scrapped, and new ones put in place.

This is happening in organisations which have carried out an objective and searching appraisal of the existing culture and found it wanting. In most instances where this has occurred two factors have been present. The first is a real sense of crisis – a genuine and widespread fear that the organisation's future survival can no longer be taken for granted. The second is the arrival on the scene of a visionary or transformational leader – a John Harvey Jones, a Colin Marshall or a John Egan in Britain, or a Lee Iacocca (Chrysler) or a Jack Welch (General Electric) in the USA – a person with the ability not only to develop a vision of the organisation's future but also to communicate it to others and inspire them with it.

[141]

Designing Organisations

The new type of culture that is developing is described in different terms by different observers. Sometimes it is called the 'organic' culture, sometimes the 'task-oriented' culture. Roger Harrison (1987) describes the process of creating it as 'a strategy for releasing love in the workplace'. The main features of companies that have transformed their cultures include the following.

- Profound respect for the individual: this is the core value associated with IBM's great success over the years. It finds its expression in training and development opportunities, greater job security, single status, etc.

- The customer is king: in British Airways the core value – putting people first – applies both to customers and to staff. In Marks and Spencer – arguably the world's most consistently successful retail operation – the customer has always been king.

- Building teams, creating networks, doing things through task forces, project groups and informal co-operation: these things are given greater emphasis; less and less use is made of traditional hierarchical structures.

- Openness and trust: sharing information, seeking feedback, using all means of two-way communication to the fullest possible extent.

- Delegation, decentralisation and autonomy: authority and responsibility are increasingly pushed down to the lowest possible levels.

- A strong emphasis on innovation: new ideas are not only welcome, they are actively sought.

- Women are treated as persons, judged on their performance and achievements and advanced accordingly.

- Above all there is an all-pervading sense of dedication to excellence and achievement. Goals are clearly stated. Above average performance is rewarded and recognised. Advancement reflects ability and performance, not seniority. Poor performers are dealt with in a caring way but not left in key positions.

This list, not surprisingly, has much in common with characteristics of winning enterprises identified by Peters and Waterman (1982) in the USA and Clutterbuck and Goldsmith (1984) in the UK. There is a growing consensus that renaissance for the Western economies is dependent on the ability of large-scale businesses to achieve cultural transformation – to leave behind the stagnant bureaucracy of the past and to develop dynamic, committed organic cultures. Toffler (1985) believes that for many famous companies it may already be too late.

The Process of Transforming Corporate Culture

On the assumption that the organisation's existing culture has been checked and found wanting, how can it be

[143]

changed? What steps can top management take to ensure that real change takes place? The evidence from company experience to date suggests the following steps are necessary.

- Develop a *mission statement* which defines the purpose for which the organisation exists. Expose this to discussion, debate and modification until it meets with general agreement.

- Develop a statement of the organisation's core values. The simpler and more easily remembered the statement the better: 'putting people first' can hardly be bettered. The temptation to develop a comprehensive list should be resisted.

- Move into detail when defining the standards of performance and the behaviours which are consistent with the values and the mission. In Avis, for example, where the values are summed up succinctly as 'We try harder', what does trying harder mean in the context of the jobs of everybody from the chief executive to the operative on the airport rental desk?

- The mission, the values and the standards should be intensively communicated, using all possible channels of communication.

- They should be integrated into training programmes and induction programmes for employees at all levels.

- The behaviour of top management, particularly the chief executive, must exemplify the new culture.

Unless role models are provided from the top the new culture is unlikely to take root.

- The decisions taken about recruiting, transfer and promotion of people must reflect the norms of the new culture. The same is true of personnel policies.

- Reinforcement must be provided in a variety of ways. Some degree of showmanship and symbolism is probably essential. Colin Marshall of British Airways was strongly criticised for spending large sums of money on changing the livery of the aircraft fleet, yet the symbolic break with the past which this represented played an important part in the transformation of the company's culture.

- It is essential to establish a system for evaluating the extent to which cultural change is actually taking place. This can be done in two ways: first, by monitoring shifts in attitudes, beliefs and values. The starting point for many programmes for cultural change is a survey to measure attitudes and beliefs of employees and/or customers. These surveys can be invaluable tools in arriving at an objective diagnosis of pre-existing corporate cultures. Their value is further enhanced if they are repeated at intervals to measure the shifts that have taken place – the shifts in both the values and beliefs of employees and the customers' perceptions of the behaviour of employees.

  A second approach is to evaluate success in terms of results. For example, British Airways set out to achieve, through changing its culture, the goal of becoming 'the world's favourite airline'. It was able to measure and feed back to employees the progress made toward this goal by reporting the position it achieved in the various world league tables compiled by travel media.

Cultural Change at London Life

One British chief executive who has given an extremely full and frank account of achieving cultural change in a highly traditional organisation is Ben Thompson-McCausland (1985), who was at the time chief executive of the insurance company London Life.

The company was founded in 1806 and had developed some strong traditions of which the management felt proud. In the 1960s and 1970s when business conditions in the financial services sector began to undergo rapid change the company came under severe pressure. The response was to cling even more strongly to the old-fashioned ways that had served it so well in the past and to seek comfort in the belief that the discriminating public would continue to place business with a company noted for its integrity and quality.

For a time, too, there was no real sense of crisis. It was true that the company was losing market share but it was not in any immediate danger of going out of business. The crisis finally arrived in 1975 when 44 per cent of the company's premium income, which came from a single source, was lost. This possibility had been foreseen for some years but no serious planning had been carried out to prepare for it.

The culture found by the new chief executive was characterised by conservatism, mistrust of innovation, complacency, inertia and a high value placed on long service, loyalty and seniority. Management ability was regarded as secondary to technical ability and 'selling' was a dirty word. Other features included a strong emphasis on consideration and caring for the staff, an easygoing attitude to work rates and performance standards and 'a sense of former grandeur'.

Thompson-McCausland took charge in 1981. He immediately set an extremely challenging goal: a growth target of 40 per cent per annum in a market growing at only 15 per cent. His initial tactics were to construct a code of values, to initiate actions which would signal the arrival of change, to gather data to illustrate the need for change and to develop expectations of achievement. His personal code of values lent themselves to the acronym THESIS:

- *Trust* – mutual trust between the chief executive and the board and between him and the employees.

- *Humility* – the requirement to try to see problems through the eyes of others and not to appear omniscient.

- *Energy* – to display an inordinate amount of energy in order to counteract the inertia present in the culture.

- *Simplicity* – to keep things as simple as possible.

- *Integrity* – to face up to issues squarely and honestly.

- *Sharing* – to share ideas as a member of a team.

The next step was to prepare both a mission statement and a corporate plan. The former was brief and to the point, containing only two statements: to sell life insurance on competitive terms and to achieve and maintain an excellent return for the members; and to become the best-run life office in the land. The first of these was a major shock in a company in which the culture was such that selling was indeed a dirty word. Other steps taken at this time included the development of new systems and procedures – particularly cash-flow budgeting – and restructuring in order to create a simpler and clearer organisation structure.

These actions were supplemented by a series of chief executive's 'walkabouts' in head office and in branches, by monthly management briefings and by considerable investment in staff training. The training programme was central to the process of bringing about cultural change. It began on each occasion with a lecture delivered by Thompson-McCausland in which he stressed the importance of people, training, personal fulfilment and genuine excellence. Workshops followed on such issues as corporate structure, communication, authority, responsibility, standards of performance and appraisal. Subsequently modules were developed on assertiveness, team-building, decision-making, time management, shared values, creative thinking and other relevant topics. Workshops took place monthly and the complete training programme was spread over two years.

The final and most crucial stage in the change process was the identification and communication of *shared values*. First, it was necessary to convince the members of the management team of the desirability of identifying values. When the subject was first raised it caused considerable embarrassment. This did not last long, however, and enthusiasm grew rapidly as the advantages of shared values became clearer. A structured interview was then conducted with each member of the management team, to raise the following questions:

- What was the culture four years ago?
- What is the culture now?
- What needs to be changed/developed?
- What is it important to retain?
- What is *your* definition of the best-run life office in the land?

The results were presented back to the management team in the form of an organisational analysis which enabled them to put substance to the abstract notions of corporate culture and shared values. Following this, and building on the responses of senior managers, a sixty-two-item questionnaire was developed and completed by ninety-one members of operating management and by employees who were members of the Staff Consultative Committee. In respect of each of the items, respondents were asked three questions: where is it at the present time, where was it a few years ago and where should it be in the future? The items consisted of pairs of statements representing opposing ends of a ten-point scale. Two examples are given below:

We are ambitious for a growth rate much higher than the industry average (left-hand side of scale).

We are satisfied with a steady increase over each previous year (right-hand side).

[149]

(N = now, B = where we were before, F = where we should be in the future.)

```
1   2   3   4   5   6   7   8   9   10
    F   N                   B
```

The type of leadership here is generally innovative.
The type of leadership here is generally to play safe.

```
1   2   3   4   5   6   7   8   9   10
    F           N           B
```

The final statement of shared values encompassed the results of the questionnaire survey, the feelings that came out of groups convened to discuss the results and requests for additional values to be added. The shared values covered the following issues:

- marketing approach;
- service;
- leadership;
- operating methods;
- people.

Thompson-McCausland's account of four years' work on changing the corporate culture ends with the comment, 'we are conscious of still being close to the start of our journey'. Nevertheless, as judged by results, the company had certainly started to move. In 1980 premium income was £39.5 million and by 1984 this had grown to £113.9 million – an increase of 188 per cent. New premiums had shown a more dramatic growth rate, of 353 per cent: from £16.3 million to £73.8 million.

The point about still being at the start of the journey remains valid, however. The main strategies for change were the training programme and the measurement and development of consensus in the area of shared values. Any attempt to have carried out these exercises in the early stages of the change process would almost certainly have been unsuccessful, given the strength and deep roots of the existing culture. The creation of trust and the building of confidence and commitment had to be carried through first, and this took time.

There are several lessons to be drawn from the London Life experience, but perhaps the most important is that real change in organisations, involving changes to strongly based cultural factors, cannot be achieved overnight or as a result of some 'quick fix' exercise. It requires a sustained programme in which the consistent commitment of top management is the essential ingredient.

Sadly, London Life subsequently encountered further difficulties, particularly following the crisis in financial markets in October 1987. It has since been the subject of a highly controversial take-over. Ben Thompson-McCausland is now chief executive of a building society. We shall hear more of him in the future.

8

Organisational Revolution

New forms of organisation are being experimented with in response to the challenges posed by a number of trends in the environment. The principal ones are the information explosion allied to the development of information technology; the increased turbulence of the economic and competitive environment; the increasing complexity of decision-making, which in turn reflects increasing specialisation married to growing interdependence of organisations; and the emergence of new sets of values concerned primarily with the quality of life for individuals and such issues as concern for the survival of 'planet earth'.

Coping with the Challenge of the Information Explosion and New Technology

Writing in the *Harvard Business Review*, Peter Drucker (1988) argues that twenty years from now the typical large business will have fewer than half the levels of management of its counterpart today and no more than a third of its managers. In its structure it will bear little resemblance to the typical manufacturing company of the past. It is far more likely to resemble organisations managers pay little attention to, such as universities, hospitals or symphony orchestras. The typical business will be knowledge-intensive, composed mainly of specialists who conduct their affairs by means of a constant two-way flow of information with their colleagues, their customers and top management. Drucker calls it the 'information-based organisation'.

Although many forces are acting together to force organisations to change, Drucker believes the development of information technology is the most powerful factor at work. In his view the organisation of the future is rapidly becoming reality. In *The Frontiers of Management* (1986) he cites as examples in the USA, Citibank, Massey-Ferguson and the Erie, Pennsylvania locomotive plant of General Electric. He makes the pertinent point that the organisation chart of the information-based system can look perfectly conventional. It behaves quite differently, however, and requires different behaviour from its members.

Information-based organisations are *flat*, with far fewer levels of management than more traditional organisations. He quotes one large multinational manufacturer which cut seven out of twelve levels of management. These management layers were not there to exercise authority, make decisions or supervise operations; their principal function was to act as 'relays' for information, rather like boosters on a telephone cable, to collect, amplify, sort and disseminate information. Modern information technology does a better job; future information technology will do an even better one – faster, more economic and more user-friendly. George

[153]

Huber (1984) paints a picture of voice-operable communications and information-processing technologies capable of coaching their users, affording the organisation's decision-makers much more information than was previously available to them. The managers that remain will *do* things (such as take decisions) rather than co-ordinate the activites of others.

A new principle, the span of communication, will take the place of the old one, the span of control. The number of people reporting to an executive will be limited only by the subordinates' willingness to take responsibility for their own communications and relationships. Control is a function of access to accurate and timely information.

Although information-based organisations need fewer managers they tend to need more specialists. These people may lack formal authority or hierarchical 'clout', and do not occupy positions in any chain of command, yet they exercise strong influence on decisions and operations, often taking control at times of crisis.

Responses to the Challenge of Turbulence and Intensified Competition

Faced with the twin challenges of an increasingly turbulent business environment and intensified global competition, organisations are being redesigned to achieve ever greater flexibility. John Atkinson (1984) points to three types of important flexibility.

The first is *functional* flexibility: the ability to redeploy employees rapidly and smoothly between tasks and activities as the nature and mix of the firm's activities change. This can involve moving multi-skilled craftsmen between electrical, mechanical and other technological systems; moving operatives on to maintenance tasks; redeploying administrative personnel into customer service and marketing functions, as happened recently on a large scale in IBM, and retraining people to exercise radically different skills. Thus, as changes occur in products, product mix, technologies and processes, the same labour force, more or less, adapts to enable it to cope, not just in the short term but over extended periods.

The second form of flexibility is *numerical*, the ability to expand or contract the headcount at short notice but without incurring the financial and social costs associated with lay-offs and redundancies. The ideal is to achieve a perfect match at any one time between the numbers of people available to the organisation and the numbers needed. The answer lies in a new model of organisation in which the traditional instrumental view of employment is abandoned and radically different employment policies can be pursued in respect of the various aspects of the organisation's activities and different categories of worker.

Permanent and stable employment will be restricted to a relatively small number of people exercising core business skills and engaged in whatever has been identified as the organisation's primary task. This core group will be expected to display a degree of functional flexibility in order to adapt to changing business conditions, but basically their ongoing tasks will involve a high degree of continuity. These are the key workers – managers, scientists, designers, technicians or marketing and sales staff.

Clustered around them, as shown in Figure 9, are other groups of workers with varying degrees of attachment to the organisation – 'loosely coupled' is the currently fashionable term. Some of these occupy the same premises as the core group and are indistinguishable from them – not only to visitors but often to other members of the organisation. They include part-time, temporary and casual workers (including in most cases a high proportion of female employees, for whom such arrangements are often ideal), who may be engaged in operational roles such as packing and assembly or supporting tasks such as administrative and secretarial work or catering. They also include self-employed subcontractors, often engaged in maintenance tasks or in specialist activities such as copywriting, software development or graphic design. On-site subcontractors are used to run whole departments – travel, catering, data processing, printing and security are obvious examples. There will also be temporary workers assigned by agencies.

The third form of flexibility is *financial*: the ability to adjust wage and salary costs rapidly (upwards as well as downwards) to respond to changes in market conditions, including competitive pressure on costs, shortages of key skills and local labour market characteristics. Financial flexibility is achieved in various ways, depending on the structure of the firm, the degree of unionisation and the balance between core and peripheral employees. Local plant bargaining makes an important contribution in unionised companies. The key to success lies mainly, however, in approaches which make it possible to adjust wage and salary costs

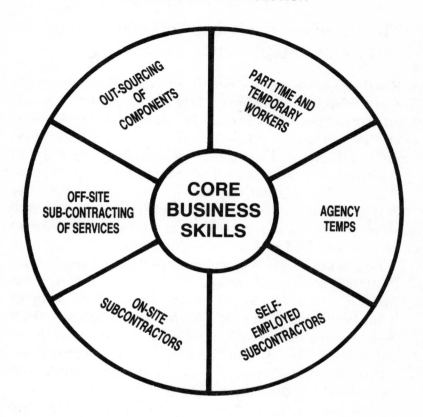

Figure 9   The flexible organisation of the future

rapidly in relation to the success or otherwise of the business. Thus, performance- or productivity-based payment schemes are preferable to those based on the rate for the job. Where profit-related bonuses form a significant part of total remuneration, flexibility is built in.

[157]

The Response to Global Complexity and Increasing Interdependence

Rosabeth Moss Kanter (1989), in *When Giants Learn to Dance*, describes three ways in which organisations are adding to their ability to compete without adding to their existing resources: pooling resources with others, allying with others to exploit opportunities, or linking systems in a partnership. The extent and range of such activities have grown rapidly in recent years, to the extent that they have become a central feature in the strategy of some companies. Kanter cites Ford, General Electric and IBM as examples of this trend.

Kanter points to a major change that has taken place in thinking about organisation. The traditional view was that the organisation existed inside a clearly defined boundary. Organisations outside the boundary, other than customers and suppliers, were actual or potential adversaries. Today the 'boundary fence' attitude is increasingly being replaced by a different concept of organisation – the edges are fuzzy and, rather like a Velcro fastener, armed with hooks which can link to other organisations for mutual advantage. Scanning the environment is as much concerned with searching for collaborators and partners as with sniffing out the competition.

In the case of Ford, a Harvard professor traced over forty coalitions between the company and other industrial or commercial organisations. In 1986 General Electric had more than 100 co-operative ventures with other firms.

In some instances organisations join forces to provide common services for members of a consortium. By 1985 there were at least forty research and development consortia in the USA. Among the most important is the Semiconductor Research Corporation, with thirty-three members including AT&T, General Motors, IBM and Du Pont, which sponsors research at several universities. In Britain a consortium of leading organisations, including Marks and Spencer and IBM (UK), was formed to sponsor joint management-development programmes for high fliers.

The relationships between organisations engaged in various forms of strategic alliance are fragile and call for careful management. Kanter quotes Corning Glass as an outstanding example of a company which has mastered the art. In 1987 about 50 per cent of Corning's profits came from over twenty partnerships. These include the Owens-Corning Fiberglas Group owned jointly with Owens-Illinois, Dow Corning jointly owned with Dow Chemical and others with Kodak, Ciba-Geigy and Plessey. From the experience of companies like Corning Kanter has reached some conclusions about what makes alliances work in the long term. She refers to them as 'the six i's'.

- The *importance* attached to the relationship is considerable; therefore adequate resources are allocated to it.

- There is agreement that the arrangement is for the long term. Thus there is *involvement*.

- The partners are *interdependent*, which keeps power balanced.

- The organisations are *integrated* so that the appropriate points of contact and channels of communication are clear.

[159]

- Each party is kept fully *informed* about the plans and intentions of the other.

- The partnership is *institutionalised* – supported by formal legal arrangements, some shared values and social relationships.

The term 'hybrid organisation' is used by Powell (1987), in an article in the *California Management Review*, to describe similar developments. Charles Handy (1984) has used the term 'federal organisation' to describe the same phenomena, while the description 'dynamic network' has been used by Miles and Snow (1986).

The characteristics of the dynamic network are:

- *Vertical disaggregation* Business activities such as product design and development, manufacturing, marketing and distribution, which 'traditionally' were carried out within a single organisation, are performed by independent organisations within a network.

- *Brokers* Business groups are assembled by or located through 'brokers'.

- *Market mechanisms* The major functions are held together by market mechanisms rather than by planning and control mechanisms.

- *Full disclosure information systems* Broad-access computerised information systems link participants in the network together in a continuously updated data bank.

For the individual company the primary benefit of participation in the network is the opportunity to pursue its particular distinctive competence. A properly balanced network can provide the degree of technical specialisation associated with a functional structure, the market responsiveness of a divisional structure and the balanced orientation of a matrix.

Companies which appear to be adopting this approach to organisation include 3M, Hewlett-Packard, Texas Instruments and Exxon.

Daniel J. Power (1988) has identified six novel forms of organisation which represent various responses to complexity. These are described in the following sections.

Hierarchical Community Structure

Two hundred or more functionally interdependent organisations will be grouped into a five- or six-level hierarchy in which individual organisations will retain a degree of autonomy. Market mechanisms, information systems and specialists in marketing, finance and planning will provide co-ordination and control. Such a large grouping of organisations will become possible as a consequence of the availability of more sophisticated management information systems and communications networks. Strategic planning would be centralised to ensure a shared view of the group's mission and strategy. However, the identity and discrete nature of each component organisation in the community and in the market place would be maintained. Performance measurement and the rewards system would be linked to the performance of each organisational unit, and stock

[161]

options would be used to encourage the best managers to stay with the community.

Two US organisations appear to Power to be heading in this direction: Allied Signal and Alco Standard. Both are conglomerates built up by acquisition, with the acquired companies usually retaining their identity and to some extent their autonomy. In Alco Standard in particular many of the component companies were previously family owned and in many cases family members continue to run their companies within the new structure.

Homogeneous, Democratic Structure

Organisations without conventional hierarchies may develop as a consequence of improvements in information technology. Small business owners and professionals could merge their businesses and use new technology to share information and resources. They would be federated organisations with power shared among the owners of the individual firms and decisions reached democratically, perhaps using computer-based voting systems. Central information systems and common software would be used to support collective action on pricing, inventory management and other decisions. In areas of professional expertise monitoring of standards and assessment of professional competence would constitute additional functions.

Examples of this structure include the US health maintenance organisations (HMOs) developed by groups of independent physicians, with each physician having his or her own private practice but receiving services from the collectively owned HMO. Another US example is the brokerage firm Prudential Bache Securities, in which the account executives essentially run their own operations under the corporate administrative umbrella. In the UK the BAT Industries subsidiary Allied Dunbar is similarly structured.

Hierarchical Replicated Structure

This involves duplicating operating divisions and co-ordinating them, again making use of new developments in information processing and communications technology. These relatively independent operating divisions can then readily be divested should the need arise. This structure would be designed to deal with diverse environments or to cope with uncertainty. Its most likely application would be in the case of companies setting up essentially similar operations in a number of different countries or operating in a similar way at several sites in a country undergoing severe economic and/or social disruption. It would be a high-cost solution since most major systems would have to be reproduced within each company.

Power (1988) quotes as an example ITT's telephone company operations, which faced very difficult environments in several foreign countries. The structural solution was to design each national subsidiary to be almost wholly independent of the parent company and easily separable.

[163]

Designing Organisations

Skeletal Multifunction Structure

This is a 'mobile' organisation, in two senses: first, it is transportable and, second, it is responsive or flexible. It involves a skeletal management team and movable or transportable production or service facilities, which can be rapidly relocated (at a cost) in response to economic or political threats or opportunities. Such an organisation would need innovations in production processes and structures to cope with rapid changes in personnel and availability of skills and with communications breakdowns. The skeletal core would need structures and mechanisms similar to those used by an army in the field.

The People Express airline had some of these characteristics. At a cost, but in a short time, it could move its base of operations or 'hub' from one airport to another.

Related Network Structure

These are best described as 'tangled structural webs'. They involve a complex combination of interlocking corporations, structural decentralisation, project teams, limited partnerships and other structural devices. They may be formed for a variety of reasons – to encourage innovation, protect investments or to make things difficult for investigative teams from regulatory institutions. Units of the organisation will have overlapping and ambiguous functions, and strategic planning in any systematic sense will be difficult.

Companies which tend to show these organisational characteristics include 'shell' companies with no func-

[164]

tion other than tax avoidance, multiple-level holding companies and other companies that for various reasons resort to complex legal mechanisms to create an organisational tangle.

Extended Hierarchical Structure

This possibility would involve stretching or extending the upper reaches of the hierarchy, with operating personnel forming a relatively small percentage of all employees. Thus spans of control would be narrow and the number of levels in the hierarchy large. Integrated information systems would hold the whole together.

Examples, Power argues, are beginning to emerge in large financial services institutions in which information technology is making it possible to automate much of the work at operations level, while an increasingly technocratic managerial bureaucracy is developing in response to growing complexity and segmentation in financial markets.

The Impact of Changing Values Systems on Organisations

Howard Perlmutter, Director of the Worldwide Institutions Research Centre, writing in *World Futures* in 1984, outlines his vision of the organisation of the future, which he calls 'the symbiotic enterprise'. It is based on a set of values, as follows:

[165]

Designing Organisations

- efficiency and international competitiveness can be consistent with concern for people as individual human beings;

- concern for wealth creation and profit can be balanced by concern for legitimacy, by the exercise of social responsibility;

- small enterprises can exist and indeed flourish in the context of large ones;

- concern for environment and non-renewable resources can be balanced with selective growth and the discovery of renewable resources;

- a wide range of technologies can be created and used, within limitations, deriving from concern about consequences;

- multi-level participation and entrepreneurial innovation can balance trends towards centralisation and increased bureaucracy;

- self-reliance on the part of individuals and communities or nations can be balanced with co-operation and partnership without descending to paternalism;

- quantity of life and quality of life can be balanced in a world in which the population is still growing;

- rights and opportunities can be tempered by acceptance of responsibilities;

- national and international disorder can be reduced through pragmatic efforts at working together taking the place of ideological confrontation.

[166]

The enterprise which reflected such a system of values would, Perlmutter argues, survive the coming challenge to the legitimacy of the traditional industrial enterprise which he believes to be inevitable, given the growing gap between the traditional sets of economic and materialist values on which enterprises have been based in the past and new concerns for individual intergrity, conservation of resources, protection of the environment and for the quality of life.

Perlmutter sees as the only possible alternative what he calls the 'anti-industrial' enterprise based on such values as 'small is beautiful', 'intermediate technology' and the beliefs that profit is immoral and co-operation produces greater benefits than competition. In Britain this alternative is well described and passionately argued for by James Robertson (1983), who calls it the 'Sane, Humane, Ecological' (SHE) organisation.

'Metanoic' Organisation

Another view of the future organisation based primarily on the impact of changing values is that of the 'metanoic' organisation. The term 'metanoic', which derives from a Greek word meaning a fundamental shift of mind, is used by Kiefer and Senge (1982) to describe what they perceive as a unifying principle underlying a range of contemporary organisational innovations: that individuals aligned around an appropriate vision can have an extraordinary impact on the world.

At the heart of the metanoic organisation is a deep sense of purpose and a vision of a desired future. The vision will, of course, vary from one organisation to

[167]

another, but the alignment of individuals around that vision is the common factor in all metanoic organisations. The resultant level of teamwork is exemplified by that found in winning sports teams, great orchestras or outstanding theatre companies. This teamwork enables the organisation to dispense with many of the traditional structural devices used to achieve control and integration.

A further shared characteristic of metanoic organisations is a consistent focus on organisation development with particular emphasis on organisation design. Companies studied by Kiefer and Senge had all implemented important innovations in organisation design.

One example of a metanoic organisation is the Kollmagen Corporation, a manufacturing enterprise in Connecticut that makes a range of products including circuit boards, periscopes, electro-optical equipment and speciality electric motors. The company has a 'small is beautiful' philosophy and is highly decentralised into divisions, each of which has fewer than 500 employees and sales of less than $50 million. There are thirteen such divisions, and the chief executive of each reports to a divisional board made up of five or six other divisional chief executives and some corporate officers. The key decisions on capital expenditure, research and development expenditure and senior management appointments remain at divisional level. Corporate staff numbers are kept below twenty-five. All employees in a division share in the profits of that division. Within divisions product teams also function highly autonomously, typically setting their own prices, determining their own sales goals and managing their own production schedules.

[168]

Organisational innovation has not stopped short at division level. At the top of the company a 'partners group' has been formed comprising the divisional chief executives and the corporate officers. The decision-making process is by consensus and each partner has veto power over any major issue.

Other US examples of metanoic organisations quoted by Kiefer and Senge include Cray Research, manufacturers of one of the world's most powerful computers, the Dayton-Hudson organisation – a large retail operation with its head office in Minneapolis – and Tandem Computer. European companies with similar characteristics would certainly include Britain's The Body Shop and Norsk Data in Scandinavia.

Conclusion

Taking all four streams of influence together it is possible to build a picture of some of the salient characteristics of organisations in the future. This has been done diagrammatically in Figure 10.

This analysis indicates a more or less convergent process – all four forces are pushing in directions which are, if not identical, at least compatible with one another. The art of organisation design in the next decade or so will lie in the ability to balance awareness of all four sets of influences. At present, different sets of experts are falling into the trap of looking at organisational issues too much from the viewpoint of a particular discipline. In consequence, information scientists concentrate on adapting organisations to the new possibilities opening

Designing Organisations

Forces making for change	Structure	Effects of these forces on:	
		Systems/procedures	Culture/values
The information explosion and information technology	Flatter structures Fewer levels of management Few direct workers More 'knowledge workers'	More flexible, more user-friendly systems More rapid transmission of timely information	More like the orchestra than the factory Knowledge and expertise more highly valued than position in hierarchy
Increased turbulence, intensified competition	Inbuilt flexibility through separation of core activities from peripheral ones	Flexible payments systems Increasing use of IT to develop 'early warning systems' to detect change Using IT to win competitive advantage	Development of strong cultural norms in core surrounded by range of sub-cultures
Complexity and interdependence	Fuzzy boundaries Complex 'tangled' structural networks Strategic alliances	Inter-organisational systems for communication and exchange of information Growing use of expert systems for problem-solving	Development of 'hybrid cultures' Balancing value placed on competition with value placed on collaboration
New systems of values	Networks replace hierarchy Influence replaces authority Autonomous work groups	Development of systems and procedures for evaluating social and human costs of organisation's activities Single-status terms and conditions of employment	Key values: Putting people first Respect of individuals Quality of life Balancing wealth creation with social responsibility

Figure 10   The organisation of the future

[170]

up as a result of developments in information technology, economists on the effects of instability and
heightened competition in markets, business strategists
on organisational complexity and how to deal with it,
while sociologists focus on the influence of changing
values and challenges to the legitimacy of large-scale
organisation.

Grasping the complexity of organisations of even
modest size, and understanding the subtle connections
between structures, systems and cultures and between
the organisational system as a whole and the forces in its
environment that are acting on it, are intellectually
demanding tasks of the highest order. To get things even
approximately right so that they work reasonably well is
a great achievement. The greatest source of comfort,
however, is the knowledge that if you do achieve this
you will generate sufficient energy, creativity and
commitment on the part of the members of the organisation to do more than compensate for any deficiences in
design.

Bibliography and References

Atkinson, John (1984) 'Manpower strategies for flexible organizations', *Personnel Management*, August.

Barham, Kevin and Rassam, Clive (1989) *Shaping the Corporate Future*, London: Unwin Hyman.

Bartlett, Christopher A. and Ghoshal, Sumantra (1989) *Managing Across Borders*, London: Hutchinson Business Books.

Beck, Michael (1989) 'Learning organizations – how to create them', *Industrial and Commercial Training*, Vol. 21, May/June.

Beer, Stafford (1972) *Brain of the Firm*, London: Allen Lane.

Boisot, Max (1987) *Information and Organizations*, London: Fontana.

Burns, T. and Stalker, G. M. (1961) *The Management of Innovation*, London: Tavistock.

Campbell, Andrew (1989) 'Does your organization need a mission?', *Leadership and Organization Development Journal*, Vol. 10, No. 3.

Clutterbuck, D. and Goldsmith, W. (1984) *The Winning Streak*, London: Weidenfeld & Nicolson.

Collard, R. and Dale, B. (1989) 'Quality circles', in Sisson (1989).

Daniels, J. D.; Pitts, R. A. and Tretter, M. J. (1985) 'Organizing for dual strategies of product diversity and international expansion', *Strategic Management Journal*, Vol. 6.

Deal, T. and Kennedy, A. (1982) *Corporate Cultures*, Reading MA: Addison-Wesley.

Department of Trade and Industry, (1985) *Quality Circles*, London: HMSO.

Drucker, Peter F. (1986) *The Frontiers of Management*, London: Heinemann.

Drucker, Peter F. (1988) 'The coming of the new organization', *Harvard Business Review*, Jan.–Feb.

Emery, F. E. and Trist, E. L. (1965) 'The causal texture of organizational environments', *Human Relations*, Vol. 18.

Emery, F. E. (1967) 'The Democratisation of the Workplace', *Manpower and Applied Psychology*, Vol. 1.

Garratt, Bob (1987) *The Learning Organization*, London: Fontana Collins.

Goold, Michael (1989) *Strategic Controls* (unpublished paper) London: Ashridge Strategic Management Centre.

Goold, Michael and Campbell, Andrew (1987) *Strategies and Styles*, Oxford: Blackwell.

Handy, Charles (1984) 'The organization revolution', *Personnel Management*, July.

Handy, Charles (1985) *Understanding Organizations*, Harmondsworth: Pelican Books.

Harrison, Roger (1987) *Organization Culture and Quality of Service*, London: Association for Management Education and Development.

Harvey Jones, John (1988) *Making it Happen*, London: Collins.

Hedberg, Bo (1981) 'How organizations learn and unlearn', in Mystrom and Starbuck (1981).

Herzberg, Fred (1966) *Work and the Nature of Man*, Cleveland: World.

Huber, George P. (1984) 'The nature and design of post-industrial organizations', *Management Science*, Vol. 3, No. 8, August.

Jewkes, J. et al. (1969) The Sources of Innovation, London: Macmillan.

Kanter, Rosabeth Moss (1989) *When Giants Learn to Dance*, New York: Simon & Schuster.

Kiefer, Charles F. and Senge, Peter M. (1982) 'Metanoic organizations in the transition to a sustainable society', *Technological Forecasting and Social Change*, Vol. 22.

Knight, Kenneth (1977) *Matrix Organization*, London: Tavistock.

Designing Organisations

Lawrence, P. R. and Lorsch, J. W. (1967) *Organization and Environment*, Boston: Harvard Business School.

McCann, Joseph and Galbraith, Jay R. (1981) 'Interdepartmental relations', in Mystrom and Starbuck (1981).

Majaro, Simon (1988) *The Creative Gap*, London: Longman.

Miles, Raymond E. and Snow, Charles C. (1986) 'Organizations, new concepts for new forms', *California Management Review*, Spring.

Miller, Eric and Rice, A. K. (1967) *Systems of Organization*, London: Tavistock.

Morgan, Gareth (1986) *Images of Organization*, Newbury Park CA: Sage.

Mystrom, P. C. and Starbuck, W. (Eds.) (1981) *Handbook of Organization Design*, Oxford University Press.

Osborn, Alex F. (1953) *Applied Imagination*, New York: Charles Scribners Sons.

Pedler, Mike, Boydell, Tom and Burgoyne, John (1989) 'Towards the learning company', *Management Education and Development*, Vol. 20, Pt. 1.

Perlmutter, Howard V. (1984) 'Building the symbiotic social enterprise; a social architecture for the future', *World Futures*, Vol. 19.

Peters, Tom (1987) *Thriving on Chaos*, London: Macmillan.

Peters, Tom and Austin, Nancy (1985) *A Passion for Excellence*, London: Macmillan.

Peters, Tom and Waterman, R. H. (1982) *In Search of Excellence*, New York: Harper & Row.

Powell, Walter W. 'Hybrid organizational arrangements: new form or transitional development', *California Management Review*, Fall.

Power, Daniel J. (1988) 'Anticipating organization structures', in J. Hage (Ed.) *Futures of Organizations*, Lexington: Lexington Books.

Price, Robert (1989) 'The decline and fall of the status divide', in Sisson (1989).

Pugh, D. (1973) 'The measurement of organization structures', in D. Pugh (Ed.) *Organization Theory*, Harmondsworth: Penguin.

[174]

Rice, A. K. (1968) *Productivity and Social Organization*, London: Tavistock.

Robertson, James (1983) *The Sane Alternative*, (privately published) Ironbridge: Robertson.

Sadler, Philip (1989) *Managerial Leadership in Post-Industrial Society*, Aldershot: Gower.

Sisson, K. (Ed.) (1989) *Personnel Management in Britain*, Oxford: Blackwell.

Smith, Adam (1922) *The Wealth of Nations*, London: Methuen.

Taylor, Frederick (1911) *The Principles of Scientific Management*, New York: Harper & Row.

Thompson-McCausland, Ben and Biddle, D. (1985) *Change, Business Performance and Values*, London: Gresham College.

Tichy, Noel M. and Devanna, Mary Anne (1986) *The Transformational Leader*, New York: John Wiley & Sons.

Toffler, Alvin (1985) *The Adaptive Corporation*, Aldershot: Gower.

Urwick, L. F. (1952) *Notes on the Theory of Organization*, New York: American Management Association.

Woodward, Joan (1965) *Industrial Organization. Theory and Practice*, London: Oxford University Press.

Index

Designing Organisations

INDEX

Designing Organisations